THE SECRET WISH OF
NANNERL MOZART

THE SECRET WISH
OF
NANNERL MOZART

by

Barbara Kathleen Nickel

SECOND
STORY
Press

CANADIAN CATALOGUING IN PUBLICATION DATA

Nickel, Barbara Kathleen, 1966-
The secret wish of Nannerl Mozart

ISBN 0-929005-89-9

1. Berchtold zu Sonnenburg, Maria Anna Mozart,
Reichsfreiin von, 1751-1829 - Juvenile fiction. 2. Mozart,
Wolfgang Amadeus, 1756-1791 - Juvenile fiction. I. Title.

PS8577.I34S4 1996   jC813'.54   C96-930384-X
PZ7.N53Se 1996

Edited by Rhea Tregebov

Cover photograph: Maria Anna (Nannerl) Mozart in formal dress.
Oil (Salzburg 1763) attributed to Pietro Antonio Lorenzoni

*Second Story Press gratefully acknowledges the assistance of
the Ontario Arts Council and The Canada Council*

Printed and bound in Canada

Published by
SECOND STORY PRESS
720 Bathurst Street Suite 301
Toronto, Canada
M5S 2R4

Contents

ACKNOWLEDGEMENTS

Sincere thanks to Sue Ann Alderson, the 1992/93 UBC Writing for Children workshop, Rhea Tregebov, Second Story Press, Cindy Nickel and her students at Shekou International School, my family, Ian Hampton, Moira Gottler, Bevan Voth, Alan Crane and Holly Duff.

for Ian,
who first introduced me to Nannerl

The Birthday Party

MARIA ANNA WALBURGA IGNATIA, Nannerl for short, caught a huge breath and closed her eyes tight.

"... beautiful purple gowns, servants, a new wig for every day of the week," she wished silently, closing her eyes tighter to help things come true faster.

"C'mon, Nannerl, blow them out before the wax gets into the cake," interrupted her brother Wolfi.

"You must make your one wish quickly, or your good luck will vanish," advised Papa.

"... a room of my own, and playing the clavier for queens in castles, and being the most famous ..." Nannerl couldn't hold her breath any longer, "the most famous composer in the whole world!" She quickly opened her eyes and with one breath blew out twelve tiny candles and the extra one Mama had placed in the middle for the year to come.

"What did you wish for?" asked Wolfi.

Nannerl sighed. Her seven and a half year old brother asked too many questions, especially about what she was thinking. She just didn't want to tell things to Wolfi any more. She would rather talk to her best friend, Katherl, who hadn't been able to come to the party because she was away on a trip. This time Mama saved her.

"It's bad luck to tell your wish," Mama explained. "You must never, ever tell it, or it won't come true."

"But what if — "

"Sh, Wolfi. We must be quiet while Papa lights Nannerl's *Zwölfjahrekerze*," whispered Mama.

Nannerl folded her arms and smiled. For once, someone had told Wolfi to be quiet because of *her*. Today was her very own special day. She watched Papa light her thick "twelve year old candle," remembering when she had been only four years old, before Wolfi was born, and the candle had been much taller. How beautiful it had been, with its swirling gold angels and violins and red roses, and its tiny black notches an inch apart all the way down the smooth wax.

That year they had burned it down to the fourth notch, and each year they had melted it down one more notch, until now the candle was only an inch high. In an hour or two it would be melted, except for a bit of old red and gold wax left in the bottom of the holder.

She sighed again. Although today was the happiest of days, with cakes and presents and even roses from Frau Spiegel, their next door neighbour, Nannerl couldn't help the ache she felt in her stomach when she thought of her candle melted down to almost nothing. "When your *Zwölfjahrekerze* has melted, you are no longer a child," Mama had told her once.

"Wolfi!" Mama's voice interrupted her thoughts.

Nannerl turned to see her brother with one finger smack in the middle of her fancy birthday cake. His blue eyes danced as he slowly drew his finger out and began to lick it furiously, like their dog Bimberl.

Nannerl couldn't help giggling. Mama finally laughed too, and sank down to her knees to stroke Wolfi's curls. He did the silliest things sometimes, but nobody stayed mad at him for long.

Mama took the silver knife and began to slice down through the sugar sprinkles and the sweet bread centre of the cake. Nannerl's stomach growled as she saw the nuts and the raisins and ... yes, Mama had remembered to add her favourite, dried apricots. And she had even used the *Gugelhupf* mould to make all those swirly patterns on the top!

But best of all were the things hidden inside; the mysterious treasures Mama mixed in the batter and baked with the cake. The things you found told your future. Nannerl hoped she wouldn't find a dumb old button this year; that would mean she'd be poor for the rest of her life.

She looked up and saw Wolfi's messy face. Crumbs and raisins fell from the sides of his mouth to the floor.

"Watch your manners, Wolfgang," Mama scolded. "The rats and the cockroaches will come out at night to eat all those raisins and ..."

"Mama, Papa, Mama!" screamed Wolfi, jumping up and down and making more crumbs fall from his mouth. He had found his treasure.

He managed to swallow his cake, then spat a button and a silver coin into his hand. "How can I be rich and poor at the same time? I'd rather be just rich," he said, looking forlornly down at the button. He threw it to the floor, and furiously polished the coin with his shirt.

Nannerl quickly ate a few forkfuls of cake, then felt a tiny object, hard against her teeth. She fished it out and held it up near the window. A thin gold ring gleamed in the sun.

"A ring!" she cried. "A ring! I've never found a ring before! Papa, what does it mean?"

"It means, dear Nannerl," Papa began, with the little smile that always made Nannerl's stomach squirm. He used that smile when he was about to tell her she had played an F instead of an F sharp, or that she had broken the rules of harmony by writing parallel fifths into her composition exercise. "It means that you will someday, most certainly, be married. And of course this prophecy will come true, and what a happy day that will be!"

Married? Nannerl tried to rearrange her wish picture, imagining a man with a red coat and shiny black shoes trailing after her through the rooms of the castle, applauding with everyone after her performances and lifting her hand high to kiss it as she curtsied. Somehow, he just didn't fit. Nannerl thought she'd rather curtsy alone.

Wolfi finished gulping down a second piece of cake and ran to Mama, who had entered the room with a basket of presents. He ran back and forth between Nannerl and Mama delivering the gifts: a hair ribbon, a new quill pen, and, Nannerl looked closer ... a small red book with a gold border around the edges.

"It's a travel diary for you to write in, on our journey," said Papa. "You must be faithful, Nannerl, and write in it every day." Nannerl held a thin white page between her thumb and index finger. The little book reminded her that in one week they would be leaving Salzburg again for another grand tour. Only this one would be even grander and longer; they might be away for three years! And of all the places she had seen, Nannerl still thought Salzburg was the most beautiful. It was just a city-state, not as big or powerful as their neighbours Austria and Bavaria. But how could she say goodbye again to the mountains and narrow, steep side streets, the twin cathedral spires and all the meandering walkways beside the Salzach River?

During the tour, she and Wolfi would perform before counts and countesses, dukes and duchesses, and all kinds of important people in the great courts. On the last tour, which had lasted a year, Nannerl had sometimes grown tired of travelling; the late nights, the smelly inns, the people with their mouths hanging open as she and Wolfi performed musical tricks like playing blindfolded. And they always seemed to like Wolfi better than her. "Look at the little boy! He's a *Wunderkind*!" they would exclaim.

But it was exciting all the same. This time they would visit Nymphenburg Palace near Munich, and cities like Coblenz along the Rhine River. Then they would go on to Paris, and Papa said he hoped that she and Wolfi could perform before the Queen and King of France at the Palace of Versailles! Nannerl felt her palms grow sweaty as she imagined curtsying to them and sitting down to play. She couldn't even imagine how big the Palace of Versailles must be, but she was sure it would be grander than any she'd ever seen.

"Listen," Papa interrupted Nannerl's thoughts. "Listen to that music. Such beautiful music, it must be Wolfi. He's slipped away to the music room. Such beautiful music, we must hear him." He dropped his fork on his plate, its clattery sound echoing in the room as everyone silently followed Wolfi's music out to the hallway, then to the music room.

Nannerl stood on her tiptoes and peered over Mama's shoulder. She noticed how small Wolfi's hands looked on the keys, how his face tightened up and his tongue stuck out a bit, and how all of his mischief had somehow dropped away from him and got into the music. It sailed up high, touching the ceiling and the portraits of Grandma Pertl, then blew through Mama's hair and out the window into the late June afternoon.

Nannerl felt the old ache in her throat, the one she always felt when she heard Wolfi play his music. It was a proud ache, but also something else, something rotten that she couldn't name. She looked at Papa's flushed face, and felt Mama's quickened breath in front of her. The feeling in her throat grew as she remembered that today was her birthday. And here they were, gawking at *him* all starry-eyed!

Nannerl couldn't stand it any more. She ran from the music room, softly so they wouldn't notice, straight to her bed in the room that she and Wolfi shared. She sobbed and sobbed into the thick quilt, until the awful ache slowly began to go away and her breath became easier to catch. She felt something in her hand. The travel diary! Maybe she could write out how she felt. She sat up, wiped her nose and eyes with her sleeve, and began to write.

June 2, 1763

Dear Diary,

    I can't stand how they pay attention to Wolfi all the time. They don't seem to care that it's my birthday, just sit around listening to him. Maybe, when I'm a famous composer, after I die, they'll find this book and everyone will read it and feel horrible about how they've treated me. I can hear Wolfi's music down the hall. Now it is finished, and they are laughing and talking and begging for more. I wonder if someday they'll beg to hear mine. Oh they will, they will! I will work on writing that Minuet and Trio I started, now! I wish Katherl would come back from Munich soon.

    Yours always,
    Anna Maria Walburga Ignatia (Nannerl)

She reached under the bed, took out a thick sheaf of papers, and sat cross-legged on the bed, determined to figure out the bothersome violin part that just wouldn't go together with the piano part, no matter how long she worked.

"Nannerl, Nannerl!" Wolfi burst through the door and began to bounce up and down on the bed, scattering her papers everywhere.

"Wolfi, just look at what you've done!"

Wolfi ignored her and kept on jumping. "Come and sing while I play the piece I wrote yesterday."

"No," she said flatly, gathering her papers and organizing them into a neat stack.

"Please, please, *please*???" he begged, and began to tickle her feet.

"All right, Wolfi, you win this time," Nannerl laughed, and shoved her compositions under the bed. She grabbed his hand and together they raced down the long hallway to the music room.

❧ 2 ❧

A Notebook for Nannerl

"... COIN ... BUTTON ... CAKE ..." Wolfi's far-off mumbles interrupted Nannerl's dream.

She opened one heavy eyelid and saw her new diary sitting on the night table. Yesterday she had turned twelve! She was now grown up, because her twelve year old candle had burned down. She ran a finger up the bony ridge of her nose and through her hair, which didn't really feel any more grown up than yesterday. Her doll, Salome Musch, smiled up at her, one eye covered with the pillow. They had named Salome after the old woman who used to come and make the meals when Mama had been sick. Nannerl sighed and kissed the doll's hard forehead. Maybe now, since she was twelve, she should stop playing with Salome and give her to Wolfi.

She looked across the room at her brother, twisted in his eiderdown quilt. He turned over and Nannerl heard the noise he made in his sleep from grinding his teeth together, then "... want ... violin ..." His words were hard to catch.

Nannerl gave up straining to hear them and snuggled down under her own warm quilt. For the fifth time in a week, she wished she had a room of her own. Wolfi's latest habit of sleep-talking kept waking her up, and this had been such a good dream. She closed her eyes and tried to make it continue. She was in a castle and the Prince had just placed a golden medallion around her neck, in honour of her great contribution to the musical life of Salzburg. She was feeling its cool smoothness against her skin, and listening to all the courtiers cheering and clapping, and ... it was no use. Nannerl couldn't go back to sleep.

She tiptoed to the hall and checked the time on the grandfather clock. Five o'clock, half an hour before Papa would come around to announce, "Nannerl! Wolfi! Time for my *Wunderkindern* to wake up and practise for their breakfast!" Wolfi usually groaned and hid under his quilt, letting Nannerl beat him to the clavier. By the time he stumbled into the music room wiping sleep out of his eyes, she was finished with her scales and ready to help Mama set out the rolls and cheese for breakfast.

She looked at the clock again. What if she practised extra long and hard today, beating Wolfi by an hour at least? Papa would be sure to praise her and say how hardworking she was, perhaps right in front of Wolfi! She went back to her room and looked at her little brother lying in his nightshirt, his quilt now kicked to the floor. Well, Papa's extra praise would help Wolfi remember he was still four and a half years younger than her. Maybe some people thought Wolfi was like God, but really he was just a little boy who liked to tickle people and sleep in.

She pulled the stiff corset over her nightshirt, feeling its achy tightness around her chest. There was no one to help her pull it tighter, but she could get Mama to do that later. She chose her new yellow dress that puffed out over her big crinoline, the one with the green bows at the sleeves and a matching bow around the cap. Papa and Mama and Wolfi sometimes teased that she was dressing up for a boy, but that was nonsense. Why couldn't she wear something nice on an ordinary day? And actually, it wasn't very ordinary. It was the day after her twelfth birthday.

Nannerl carefully closed the door of the music room so that she wouldn't wake anyone up. Her fingers felt cold and stiff as they went up and down the keys, playing scales and arpeggios over and over until the sky turned pink and the birds woke up and joined her with scales of their own. Nannerl stopped suddenly. Had she heard Mama and Papa's door click open? She wanted to play something for Papa, something that would be a secret just between the two of them.

She noticed a thin notebook sitting on top of a messy stack of papers. The inscription on the worn front cover, in Papa's clear hand, read: *For the clavier, this Notebook belongs to Miss Maria Anna, 1759.* She had forgotten about the notebook, thought it was sitting somewhere at the back of the old music cupboard. How had it got here? It was the one Papa had given to her at her first clavier lesson, when she was seven.

Nannerl flipped through the book. Most of the early pieces were minuets composed especially for her by Papa. She found her favourite, Minuet No. 11, and began to play. Maybe Papa would hear it and remember the lesson when she had played it for him. That time she had played it without any mistakes, but also with something else. She had put everything into the music: Mama's hugs and the way Wolfi made her laugh, chocolates, their dog Bimberl's fur and the shadows that flicked over the walls during supper. She had stirred all of it into the little minuet so that it steamed rich like the stew Mama made on winter afternoons.

"You are an amazing talent, my daughter Maria Anna," Papa had whispered, and Nannerl could tell he was serious because he used her formal name. Two tears had slipped silently from his eye to the clavier keys. After that she'd played the minuet over and over for two weeks, until one evening Mama had stormed into the room and told her to please play something else because she was going crazy.

A small click interrupted Nannerl's thoughts. She stiffened. Papa had opened the door and was standing there listening to her play! Her heart beat harder but she kept on until the final note, trying to play the way she had on the day Papa had cried. When she was finished, she felt his hand on her shoulder and turned around quickly to see if he was pleased. He was smiling.

"You're up early, Nannerl! What a diligent, hard-working daughter I have, playing so beautifully at six o'clock in the morning," he said, sitting down on the bench beside her.

Nannerl's fingers tingled with the praise. Being with Papa alone was even better than being praised in front of Wolfi. She loved Papa's soapy smell and the way his coat brushed against her dress.

"You played this piece superbly when you were only seven," Papa reminisced. He had remembered! "Do you recall when you used to play this again and again and drove your poor Mama crazy?" he asked, and they both laughed. "Let's play it together, just for fun." Nannerl nodded and quickly turned the page back before Papa could change his mind. He hardly ever did things just for fun.

"Wait, Nannerl!" Papa turned to the last page of the

piece again. "Can you read what I wrote here, at the end of the piece?"

Nannerl peered closer to read Papa's tiny script. *This minuet and trio little Wolfgang learned in half an hour on 26th January, 1761, one day before his fifth birthday, at half past nine at night.* She had forgotten that, although this notebook had first been hers, Wolfi had later learned all of the pieces perfectly. Papa had carefully recorded Wolfi's progress after each piece.

She looked up. Wolfi stood in the doorway, rubbing his eyes. He came over, looked at the notebook, and suddenly wasn't sleepy any more. He snatched it from the piano ledge and started skipping around the room.

"I found this in the old cupboard," he sang, panting and returning to the clavier, "and I'm using the empty pages at the back to write music. See, Papa," he turned the pages and held up a fresh composition, "I composed this sonata movement last week!"

"Well, well, we must hear it," said Papa with a smile. He stood up. "Here, Wolfi, play it for us."

Nannerl thought she would explode. She stood up.

"It's my book!" she cried. "Papa gave it to me and it's mine! You're always taking my things!" She glared at Wolfi.

"But, Nannerl," Papa said, "you must be reasonable. You haven't used this book for years. It was just sitting in the cupboard. I see no harm in Wolfi using it for his compositions."

"You just don't understand," Nannerl cried, running from the room. "It's not fair!"

Papa called after her but Nannerl didn't really hear and she didn't care either. She slammed the door and sank down onto the bed and began to sob, then remembered that she had cried here last night too.

"I'm supposed to be twelve and grown up and all I can do is cry," she thought, as Wolfi's sonata drifted out from the music room. She dug her fingers into the quilt, smelling coffee and fresh rolls that made her stomach growl. She would stay here all day. That would show them. Not that they'd really care if she starved.

Mama knocked at the door. Nannerl could tell it was her, because Papa or Wolfi would have just barged right in.

"Come in," Nannerl said into her quilt.

"It's time for breakfast," Mama said in her no-nonsense voice. "You're not going to stay up here and starve over a notebook, so you might as well blow your nose and get something to eat. Let me tighten your corset first." Nannerl knew there was no sense in arguing with Mama. She slowly stood up and allowed herself to be fixed. She hated how the corset squeezed, even when she was playing the clavier or running up the hill to the market for eggs.

At breakfast and during the arithmetic lesson that

followed, Wolfi tried to make Nannerl laugh by making faces at her behind Papa's back. His crabby neighbour Frau Spiegel face almost succeeded, but she managed to hide behind a book so he wouldn't see her smile.

After dinner, Nannerl found the notebook on her chair. Wolfi looked straight at her, his eyes begging for a truce. She lifted the notebook, nodded, and gave him a queenly smile, sort of lofty and far off. Wolfi drummed a riddle with his knuckles in their secret code language; two quarter note taps, a triplet, two half notes and four sixteenths, meaning "What looks like a noodle?" She shrugged. He made his Frau Spiegel face again and this time Nannerl burst into a loud giggle.

Papa turned around and glared at them. He often looked that way, now that the Grand Tour was so close. "Come here, both of you," he ordered. Nannerl braced herself for a lecture. Wolfi came around and sat on Papa's lap and she leaned against the table.

"In less than a week we depart for Munich," he said in a brisk voice. "You two will be in the spotlight, and the eyes of many distinguished people will view you. You will be earning money, just like adult musicians. This is serious business, and you must act like professionals. Wolfi, what's a professional?"

"Um ... it's like an adult, I guess," he said, "an adult who has a job and receives money."

"Good," said Papa, "except that you don't have to be an adult to be a professional. Now, Wolfi, why the long face? Remember the rewards! Remember the way people clapped? Remember when you sat on the lap of the Empress Maria Theresa of Austria? Think of the opportunity! Perhaps on this tour the great Johann Christian Bach will hear your compositions!"

Johann Christian Bach, son of Johann Sebastian Bach! One of the greatest composers alive! Nannerl imagined sitting at the clavier with the great composer while he played her latest composition. He would pat her on the back and say in a gruff voice, "Well done, my girl. I must see about getting this published immediately!"

A loud knock echoed through the apartment.

"There's my first student," said Papa. "Now finish your work quietly, and remember that you are both professionals."

That evening after supper, Wolfi begged Nannerl to play "March Around and Play the Violin" with him but she said no, partly because she couldn't really play the violin and partly because she had important work to do. She shut the door to their room, got out her diary, and lay on the bed. Bimberl panted and jumped up beside her and Nannerl stroked the dog's fur while she wrote.

June 3, 1763

Dear Diary,

I'm so excited about the Grand Tour! Papa says we might play for the great Johann Christian Bach! And I have a plan! My plan is to have a new piece of music finished perfectly so that I can play it for him and he'll help me become famous, maybe even help me to get it published! But what should I compose? It will have to be something brand new, something no one has ever heard. I'll make it as big as the sky but quiet sometimes too, like the candlelight shadows dancing across this page ...

Nannerl felt her eyelids grow heavy and she jerked suddenly, catching herself dozing. Bimberl slept soundly beside her. She could hear Wolfi march around the house, still playing his violin. She fell asleep with his music ringing in her ears.

3

THE SECRET SYMPHONY

IN, OUT, PULL. IN, OUT ... Nannerl sewed in rhythm to
the tune that she hummed — softly, so Mama wouldn't
hear. She glanced across the big kitchen to the fireplace
where Mama stood pouring the wax to make candles.
Nannerl hummed the tune again, but in her head this
time. This wasn't any old tune. It was the tune of a symphony! Her symphony! The one she was going to have
finished by the time she met Johann Christian Bach!

Nannerl had spent every extra minute of the past four
days composing. It wasn't easy. When she wasn't practising
the clavier, she was helping Mama wash the clothes, bake
the bread, make the soap and pack the trunks for the trip.
When she did manage to slip away to her room, someone
would always barge in with a question or an errand. So
far, no one had discovered her secret. She had become an
expert at slipping her papers under the bed and pretending to knit as soon as she heard the door click.

Nannerl knew what would happen if Papa discovered
that she was composing a symphony. She remembered

when she had tried to show him her sonata for violin and piano. First, he would laugh. Then he would shake his head and say, "A symphony, Nannerl! Where did you ever get such an idea? To compose a symphony, one must have years and years of strict training and besides, you musn't waste your time with such things. There is so much music already written for you to practise. And there are so many household tasks that you must learn from your Mama!" Then, to make her feel better, he would give her a few little composition exercises. Baby things, like filling in chords to a bass and melody line already given! As if she hadn't already done that when she was eight!

Now if her symphony were published ... what would Papa say then? Inside her head, Nannerl could hear the sound of forty, maybe fifty violins, rising above the deep voices of the cellos. It would have more instruments than any symphony anyone had ever written. She could hear them swirling together, surrounded by flutes and an oboe and —

"Nannerl!" Mama's scolding voice interrupted the entrance of the clarinets. "Stop your dreaming and get on with the sewing! There are trunks to pack and clothes to iron and bread to bake. We're leaving tomorrow, not next year!"

"Sorry, Mama," said Nannerl, stabbing the rose-coloured satin with her needle. Her best performance dress, with all its gold embroidery and silk lace, lay in a heap on the kitchen table. Nannerl sighed and checked how much lace was left to attach to the sleeve.

It seemed that the lace had always been her monthly job. First, she had to take it all off, or it would be ruined in the wash. Then, after the washerwoman had scrubbed the clothes, and after the drying, the lace all had to be stitched on again. Nannerl had been sewing lace on her and Mama's clothes for the last two weeks!

Now there was just one row of stitching left. In, out, pull. In, out, pull ... Nannerl's sewing needle moved back and forth, conducting the music in her head like a baton. Suddenly, moist, warm fingers covered her face, and satin brushed the back of her neck.

"Guess!" said a familiar voice behind her.

"Katherl, of course, you silly goose!" said Nannerl, standing up and hugging her best friend. Katherl's father was the Salzburg court surgeon. Since Papa was assistant court composer, Nannerl and Katherl had always been friends.

Nannerl looked at Katherl's dress. It completely covered her feet. Nannerl had begged Papa to buy her a "grown-up" dress that was really long like thirteen year old Katherl's. But Papa wouldn't hear of it. He disapproved of very long dresses. "She's always trailing dirt," he would say. Today, as usual, the bottom of Katherl's dress was splotched with mud.

"Good afternoon," said Katherl, curtsying and turning to Mama. "I hope you don't mind that I didn't knock. Your servant, who was outside preparing the carriage, let me in, so I thought I'd surprise Nannerl."

"Good afternoon, Maria Anna," said Mama, smiling at Katherl over the candle wicks. Katherl's real name was Maria Anna Katharina, almost the same as Nannerl's.

Nannerl lifted her needle. "Isn't it exciting about Sebastian?" she said. "He's our very own servant, and we have our own carriage too! Even if we are hiring the driver and horses in stages. On the last tour we had to ride in a public carriage and it was horribly squished."

"Sebastian is handsome. How old is he?"

"Oh, I don't know. Probably about nineteen. How was your trip to Munich? Did you get a new bonnet?"

"Two. You should see them. The new fashion is to have a few flowers above the rim, sweeping down like ... so ... just above the eyes. I will be the first in Salzburg to show it off," said Katherl, fingering the lace on Nannerl's performance dress. "What I wouldn't give for a dress like this! Was it really a present from the Empress Maria Theresa?"

"Of course," said Nannerl, remembering that performance when she and Wolfi had astonished the court in Vienna. The next day, the paymaster had come to the inn where they were staying and delivered two costumes; one for Wolfgang, the other for her. Whenever she put it on for a performance, Nannerl would finger the edges of the lace, feeling lucky and grown up.

She pulled the last stitch with a tug. "Finished!" she announced, glancing over at Mama. "Could I please say goodbye to Katherl, just for a few minutes?"

Mama looked up from the candles with her lips pressed together, but Nannerl detected the trace of a smile. "Well, just for a few minutes. But watch the time carefully ... there are clothes to iron and trunks to pack and — "

" — bread to bake," Nannerl finished as she grabbed Katherl's hand and raced out to the hall.

Outside the music room, Nannerl pressed her ear against the closed door, motioning for Katherl to do the same.

"Wolfi, here is the score of a symphony by Joseph Haydn. Notice the instruments he chooses," Papa's voice drifted out with a few notes played on the violin.

"C'mon Nannerl, let's — " whispered Katherl, but Nannerl just shook her head and listened harder. So Papa was teaching Wolfgang how to write a symphony! "You must know the sound of each instrument very well," Papa continued, "so that you know which ones will sound right together. You choose a theme, a melody as a basis, then expand upon it." Some clavier notes drifted out to the hall.

Nannerl pressed her ear hard against the door until it almost hurt, as if that could somehow help her to be in there with Wolfi and Papa. She didn't want to miss anything. But it seemed as if Papa wanted to keep leaving her out.

Well, she would just have to work harder. Maybe tonight, after the packing. Who needed lessons from Papa anyway? She had studied that score a hundred times at least, in the mornings before she practised the clavier.

She and Katherl tiptoed to her room, trying not to step on the creaky parts of the floor. Nannerl closed the door and Katherl sat down on the bed. She sighed. "Do you realize that you are the luckiest girl in Salzburg? What I wouldn't give to visit Paris and London and Amsterdam!"

"With only your Mama and Papa and little brother for company?"

"But just think who you might meet! Your new servant Sebastian seems nice. When did your Papa hire him?"

"Just the day before yesterday, for the trip." Nannerl paused. "Katherl ... if I show you something very secret, will you promise not to tell anyone?"

Katherl kneeled on the floor. She lay her head on the bed and closed her eyes. "Never, ever," she said in solemn tones. "I promise, and if I do, death shall be my punishment."

"Get up, you silly goose," said Nannerl, giggling. "All right, here it is." She quickly thrust the stack of papers at Katherl, then looked at the floor with her hands behind her back.

"Is it a sonata?" asked Katherl.

"No."

"A trio?"

"No."

"A quartet?"

"No, silly, look at the number of instruments!" Nannerl looked up from the floor. Her friend's mouth dropped open.

"A ... a symphony? You're writing a symphony?" asked Katherl in her loudest voice, the one that always seemed to fill a room to the very top.

"Sh!" said Nannerl. "No one can find out, until I can get Johann Christian Bach to help me get it published. It's going to be gigantic. It'll have way more instruments than any symphonies now, perhaps hundreds of them! I think it'll even have a boys' choir and an adult choir and ... oh, Katherl, what do you think?"

Katherl studied the music and Nannerl waited, twisting a loose bit of thread around her finger. Katherl took clavier lessons sometimes. It wasn't as if she knew as much about music as Papa or anything, but Nannerl still felt nervous.

"Well?" asked Nannerl, still twisting the bit of thread. Katherl quickly looked up. "It looks fine, but — "

"But what?"

"Well ... um ... all those instruments ..."

"You don't like it? You think it's a stupid idea?" Nannerl pulled the thread against her fingertip, indenting the skin.

"No, no, I like it. But what I mean to say is ... well ... nobody's ever written anything with so many instruments. Maybe it's kind of ... well ... kind of big?"

"Maybe ..." said Nannerl. She swallowed the lump in her throat.

"Anyway, I think you're a genius!" said Katherl in a loud voice, so that Nannerl had to shush her again. "Sorry," Katherl whispered. "People will probably think it sounds strange. But who cares what they think, as long as you know it's the best thing you ever wrote!"

"I don't know," said Nannerl. "I think I'd like it to be published and be famous."

"Well, I hope you do get to be famous. You deserve it, because you work so hard and you're so talented. Papa says you and Wolfi are the greatest performers in all of Europe!"

"Always performer ... I wish they would say composer," said Nannerl, looking down at her symphony. She lifted her head and looked at Katherl. "Do you think some day they will?"

"I know they will!" said Katherl. She noticed the thin book lying on Nannerl's night table and picked it up. "What's this?"

"It's a travel diary, to write in every day. Will you write to me? Maybe you could even send ideas for the symphony with Herr Hagenauer's letters."

"Who's Herr Hagenauer?"

"Our landlord, silly. Remember — he owns the grocery shop next door? And he has a daughter, the stuck-up one who thinks she's so great just because she's fifteen? Herr Hagenauer and Papa always write letters when we're away, so you could send your letters and ideas with his! And I'll send letters with Papa's!"

Katherl kneeled again, with her hand outstretched this time, like the actor in the French theatre group Nannerl had seen in Vienna.

"Dearest Nannerl," she whispered, "I shall write thee always, faithfully, and I shall never, ever, forget thee."

Nannerl giggled, but deep in her stomach she felt an ache. Three years! How could she live without Katherl for three years! She grabbed the outstretched hand and lifted the older girl to her feet.

"I'll miss you," said Nannerl, hugging her friend and not wanting to let go.

Wolfi suddenly marched into the room. "Mama's getting mad at you for staying away so long," he reported.

"She says you should come right away, to iron the clothes. She says we're leaving tomorrow, not — "

" — next year," finished Nannerl, giving Katherl one final hug.

Wolfi stuck his tongue out at Katherl. "Catch me if you can, but don't trip over your long dress," he said, running away.

Katherl started to run after him, then stopped. Their latest trick in dealing with Wolfi was to ignore him. She and Nannerl stepped into the hall in their most dignified manner. They linked arms and whispered all the way to the front door.

"Goodbye, dear Nannerl, goodbye," Katherl said, blowing kisses as she walked backwards and bumped into Sebastian, who was coming in from outside. She blushed.

"Bye, dearest Katherl," said Nannerl, blowing a steady stream of kisses to her friend. She felt like crying but she couldn't, not yet, not in front of Sebastian.

"Nannerl!" Mama's voice came out from the kitchen.

"Bye!" Nannerl said again, waving and watching Katherl lift her long dress and stumble down the stairs.

Nannerl ran to the kitchen. She watched Katherl step onto the cobblestone street below. The ache was in her throat as she began to press Wolfi's suit. Three years without Katherl. Two hot tears fell on the cloth and sizzled under the iron as she moved it back and forth, back and forth. Then the violins in her head tuned up and began to play, and she started to feel the rhythm again, the rhythm of the symphony she shared with Katherl.

⤐ *4* ⤏

*G*OODBYE!

*N*ANNERL WOKE UP and shivered. She kneeled on her bed to look out the window at the dark morning, and saw mist hovering around the streetlights and the fountain in the square below. The women wouldn't come to draw water for another few hours. Everyone was still sleeping. Only the grandfather clock in the hall clicked into the silence. Nannerl crept out of bed to check the time — two o'clock. They would be leaving in an hour and a half.

She tiptoed to the kitchen, feeling the cold floor on her bare feet. She would make breakfast and surprise Mama. She lay out the sticks for the fire, feeling a clutch at the bottom of her stomach when she thought of leaving Salzburg for ... for what? All the people and places seemed blank as the morning and the mist. She tried not to think about Katherl as she put out the hard bread and cheese, turned the handle of the coffee grinder and listened to the crunch of the coffee beans. The violins in her head wouldn't wake up and play her symphony tune. She heard the click of her mother's shoes instead.

"Nannerl, you'll catch a cold with your bare feet on this floor. Go and change, then wake your brother and come back for breakfast."

"But I'm not hungry," protested Nannerl.

"You'll eat your breakfast just the same," said Mama, as she took over the grinding. "I'll not hear a single growling stomach until Munich."

"Yes, Mama," Nannerl said as she ran to her room. Wolfi was still asleep with his quilt kicked off, curled up like a puppy. Nannerl sat down on his bed and ran her fingers through his curls. "Wake up," she whispered. "Wolfi, wake up. Hurry and get ready! We're leaving soon!"

Wolfi rubbed his eyes. "Bimberl!" he said. "Who will take care of Bimberl?"

"Oh, Wolfi. Don't you remember? Herr Hagenauer of course!"

Nannerl picked up the corset that was lying across her trunk and began to pull it on. She turned her back to Wolfi so that he could lace it up. "Ouch!! Not so tight! I'd like to see you wear a corset!"

"No, thanks," said Wolfi, picking up Salome Musch from under his quilt and hopping out of bed. Two days ago, Nannerl had given Salome to Wolfi, and now the old doll slept on his bed. "I hope there's enough room for Salome Musch."

Nannerl looked at the tiny cracks around the edges of

Salome Musch's mouth. She remembered the horrible day the doll had gone missing. It had been a week before Bimberl had found her behind some flowers in the backyard garden during a game of lawn bowling. Nannerl reached for the doll. "Maybe I should take care of Salome for a while, just until we're safely on our way. So she doesn't get hurt."

"Wolfi! Nannerl! Come and get your breakfast, before the coffee gets cold!" called Mama.

Bimberl met them in the hall and trotted after them to the kitchen with her tongue hanging out.

"Mama, poor Bimberl is hungry," said Nannerl, as she and Wolfi entered the kitchen.

"Herr Hagenauer will have food for her, I'm sure," said Papa. "Now sit down and eat, children. We must depart at precisely three-thirty, if we are to arrive in Munich by nightfall." He inspected his travel schedule. While Mama packed the lunch, Nannerl passed a few tidbits of cheese and bread down to Bimberl.

After breakfast, Wolfi and Nannerl watched the hired driver load the trunks into the boxes on either side of the carriage. They shivered in their grey travel capes as Papa and Herr Hagenauer went over the final arrangements, talking in low voices about money. She waited until they were finished, trying to get up enough courage to ask Herr Hagenauer about Katherl.

"Excuse me, Herr Hagenauer," said Nannerl. "But do you think my friend Katherl could send letters with yours? She could give them to you at Mass and — "

"Nannerl," interrupted Papa, "we musn't inconvenience Herr Hagenauer."

"No problem, my dear girl, no problem at all," said Herr Hagenauer. "Katherl's the one with the long dress, yes?"

"Yes," said Wolfi, tripping over his own feet in an imitation of Katherl.

The University Church clock struck the half hour. It was three-thirty. "Come along children, we really must leave now," said Papa.

Bimberl began to jump up and down and bark, licking Nannerl and Wolfi's legs. They got to their knees, kissed her and stroked her fur. "Goodbye, dear Bimberl," said Nannerl.

"Wolfi! Nannerl!" Mama called.

They walked slowly to the carriage. Bimberl whined and turned in circles. Nannerl tried not to feel the ache as she climbed inside. Then Sebastian closed the door, the driver gave the horses a whip and they started down the street, away from the square. Nannerl pressed her nose against the window and waved at Bimberl and Herr Hagenauer, at their building with its rows of windows, at the tip of the University Church peeking up from behind. The carriage turned the corner.

Wolfi snuggled down against Mama's shoulder and began to sleep. Nannerl sat up straight; she realized that she was clutching Salome Musch so tight that her hands hurt. She looked around, hoping no one would see her holding a doll as if she were a little girl. But everyone was sleeping except Papa, who probably wouldn't notice anyway.

Salzburg was turning blue. Goodbye, town square, with your musicians and your marionettes and your people selling sausages! Goodbye, fortress way up high on the hill! The horses clopped over the bridge. Nannerl craned her neck to look back at the mountains, giant black shapes in the blue light. She memorized how the spires of the nunnery and the Franciscan Church poked the sky. Then she leaned back in her seat as the carriage strained up a steep hill. Goodbye, Katherl! Goodbye, Bimberl! Nannerl squeezed Salome Musch until the buildings and cobblestone streets turned to waving fields, the faint pink light of day crept around the edge of the sky, the birds woke up chattering and the horses' hooves clopped in her dreams.

❧ 5 ❧

An Organ and a Broken Wheel

Nannerl woke to a huge thump. She rubbed her eyes and saw that the carriage wasn't moving, and that everyone but Wolfi and she was outside on their knees, inspecting something. She shook Wolfi awake and hurried out. Papa was scowling. Mama's lips were tight, her arms crossed. Nannerl looked under the carriage — the back wheel lay in pieces.

"Thank God we've got fine weather," said Sebastian, trying to sound optimistic and looking up at the sky.

Papa consulted the map. "At least we've crossed into Bavaria. I'd say we're two hours outside the town of Wasserburg," he said. "It's the next town between here and Munich. Over that hill is a mill. Perhaps they will help us. Sebastian and I will walk over and see what can be done. Wolfi and Nannerl, stay out of your Mama's way."

While Wolfi begged Mama to help him find his violin in the carriage box, Nannerl searched through the

· 46 ·

ditch for wild June roses. When she found a few, she spread her cape on the grass and sat on it. She loved the sun on her hair, and the way the clouds looked like pieces of wool before spinning. The buzz of bees mingled with the sound of Wolfi's violin. Nannerl sighed. If only she could really play, too.

Sometimes she'd sneaked Wolfi's violin to try it out — but Papa had never taught her. Girls didn't play the violin or the organ. She had asked Papa why. "Nannerl," he'd said, "You are a very lucky girl to be able to learn the clavier and to sing. That is enough, and you should be grateful. You have no need of the violin or the organ; they are only necessary if one is to have a job as the director of music in a court or church. And those are jobs for men ... your job is to find a husband!"

She pulled out a few blades of grass and tore them up. Sometimes Papa just didn't make sense. Someday, maybe, years and years in the future, she might want a husband. But why should that keep her from learning the violin right now? It would be so much easier to write for an instrument that she could play. But then, she wasn't really supposed to compose either, except for those tiresome exercises Papa always gave her.

Papa and Sebastian and two men from the mill returned with a wheel. "It looks a little small and the hub is long, but we can try," said one of the men. Nannerl got up and watched as they cut down a small tree to hold the wheel in place, then fit it on and attached the iron hoop from the other wheel under the carriage box.

"I believe we're ready to go," said Papa, wiping sweat and dust from his forehead with a handkerchief. "About time!" He looked at his pocket watch. "We've wasted almost an hour on this road. We won't make it to Munich tonight. We'll have to stay over in Wasserburg. Children, you and Mama will travel by carriage. Sebastian and I will walk the rest of the way to Wasserburg. We don't want to add extra weight or that wheel will break."

Nannerl got in behind Wolfi and Mama. They all waved to Papa and Sebastian, who plodded after them down the dusty road. Nannerl wrote in her diary about the broken wheel, and it didn't seem long before she looked up and saw the big square church tower above the buildings of the town. They were like Salzburg buildings — high and narrow and pressed together, as if they were rubbing shoulders, looking out over the bridge and the river and the boats.

"Is it Wasserburg?" asked Wolfi, who had been singing and writing music.

"Yes, and thanks to God we've made it without another breakdown. The driver will take us straight to the smith to fix our wheel," answered Mama. "Look, there's the inn!"

When they reached the blacksmith's, Wolfi hopped out of the carriage.

"C'mon Nannerl, I'll race you to the inn!" he said and ran off. Nannerl tried to catch him, but he got there before her. When she walked into the dim front room, out of breath, Wolfi was already asking the innkeeper for a room.

"And just who are you, little man?" asked the innkeeper, laughing.

"I'm Wolfgang Amadeus Mozart, and this is my sister, Nannerl," answered Wolfi in his most dignified voice.

"The Mozart children! I've read all about you in the papers! And where are your parents?"

"Oh, they're coming soon," answered Nannerl. "Maybe we can find a room and surprise Mama."

"Follow me," said the innkeeper, and led them up a dusty stairwell to a tiny, hot room. He opened the window. "See, you have a view of the church across the street."

Nannerl and Wolfi ran to the window and stuck their heads out, looking at the huge church with its massive square tower. Mama and the driver walked slowly up the street towards the inn.

"Mama!" called Wolfi, and they looked up.

"So that's where you children are!" said Mama. "We thought you had been kidnapped! And you got us a room, all by yourselves!" Nannerl was glad that Mama wasn't angry. She felt in the pocket of her cape for the diary, and began to finish the entry she had started in the carriage, dated June 9, 1763.

... and then Papa came from the mill with another wheel for the carrij. They —

"You spelled carriage wrong," said Wolfi, looking over her shoulder. It's spelled c - a - r - r - i - a - g - e."

Nannerl blushed and snapped the book shut. Only Wolfi got spelling and grammar lessons from Papa. "How dare you read my diary? You're always snooping around in everything that's mine!" she said. She looked out the window, feeling hot and tired. Two familiar figures walked down the far end of the street.

"Papa! Sebastian!" cried Nannerl. She turned to Mama. "May I run down to meet them?"

"Yes, but don't trip over the stairs," Mama warned from the bed where she was resting. But Nannerl was already racing down the stairs with Wolfi at her heels. She wanted to be the first to greet Papa. Maybe he would pick her up, the way he used to when she was little. She ran across the square, dodging bakers and children, dogs and wagons. She noticed Wolfi's curls flying a few feet in front of her. If only she didn't have this dress and this corset! They kept getting in the way. Her legs hurt from running so fast. She looked ahead and saw that Wolfi was already in Papa's arms. She slowed down.

"That was a snail's journey," Papa was saying as Nannerl caught up.

"Papa, can you explore the church with us, please, please, please?" begged Wolfi.

"We must see the smith and the cartwright first," said Papa, putting Wolfi down and taking his hand. "Then we will explore the church."

Nannerl followed them to the smith's shop, out of breath. Her dress felt tight and all the layers stuck to her skin. She wished she was home in her room, with Katherl.

Finally, Papa was ready to see the church. The doors creaked as they let themselves in. The dark, musty air felt cool on Nannerl's skin as they walked slowly down the aisle. They looked up and back to the balcony. The organ! Streams of dusty light came in through the stained glass and fell on the row of huge, gleaming pipes.

"Papa, I've never played an organ!" Wolfi was jumping up and down. "Could I play it, please, please, please, Papa?"

The priest walked towards them down the long aisle, twisting his hands and frowning.

"Good afternoon, Father," said Papa. "We were just looking at your beautiful organ. I am Leopold Mozart, and these are my children, Wolfgang and Nannerl."

The priest's frown turned to a smile as he looked at

Wolfi. "You are the *Wunderkind*, Wolfgang Amadeus, from Salzburg?"

"Of course," said Wolfi. "May I try playing your organ please? I've never played an organ before."

"Certainly," said the priest, and led them up the creaky back stairs to the balcony. When they reached the organ loft, Papa began to show Wolfi how to use the pedal. Nannerl peered over Papa's shoulder and watched closely as his foot pressed gently on one of the wooden pieces sticking out from the bottom of the huge instrument. "You put your foot down like this to make the sound," he started to explain, but Wolfi was already pushing away the stool and trying the keys. The sound thundered into every corner of the great church.

Nannerl studied Wolfi's hands as they worked the keys and pushed and pulled at the stops. She watched his feet dance over the pedals. Then she closed her eyes and let it all wash over her, like the huge waves she imagined crashed against the shores of the Baltic Sea. Finally she opened her eyes and saw Wolfi's curls bobbing barely above the second row of keys.

When he stopped playing Nannerl could still feel the vibrations in the banister of the balcony. Papa and the priest crowded around Wolfi in silence, their eyes wide.

Papa finally spoke. "This is indeed a fresh act of God's grace," he sputtered, with his hands on Wolfi's head. "Anyone else would take months of practice to play the organ with such skill." They all started to talk at once and walked from the organ loft with Wolfi.

Nannerl hung back, staring at the organ. Her fingers ached to reach out and fill the church with music. She brushed one key with her fingertip. She wanted to sit and play for as long as she wished, with no one around to stop her or say it wasn't proper. She touched another key. Then she had an idea. She fiddled with it for a while, stroking the back of her hand up and down the keys, lightly, so they wouldn't make a sound. Her heart thumped in her ears.

It was still thumping late that night as she lay in bed beside Wolfi, watching the moonlight fall in pools on the quilt. She had been tossing and turning for hours. The family had gone to bed early, in hopes of getting a good start in the morning if the carriage was ready. Nannerl turned again. Should she follow her plan? She kept hearing two notes. One was sweet as birdsong. The other had something steely about it, an organ sound. The two notes clashed and Nannerl shoved her head under the pillow, not knowing which one to hear. Then the organ sound took over, and she suddenly knew what she had to do.

She quietly got out of bed. That part was easy. She was used to creeping around without waking anyone. She pulled on her dress and cape and tiptoed out of the room and down the stairs, holding Salome Musch tight to her chest.

Bright moonlight lit the quiet street. Nannerl slowly crossed the cobblestones, opened the church door just a crack and slipped inside. Shivers crisscrossed her skin as she climbed the dark balcony steps. Maybe the ghost of St Paul hid in the corners, shaking a bony finger at her! He would surely disapprove of her sneaking around the church at night like a thief! What if the priest caught her? Then the huge organ pipes rose high above her and Nannerl forgot about ghosts. She propped Salome Musch on a little shelf of the organ, pushed the stool away as Wolfi had done, and began to play.

After a while it seemed as if she had always done this. It was like eating an apple or threading a needle. The great sound filled her head, spilled out of her ears and mixed with the moonlight all around her. She forgot about tight corsets and Papa's squirmy smile and mis-spelled words. She pulled out all the stops, listened to the music rumble through the church.

Something made her stop. Silence filled her ears, broken suddenly by a creak. She turned and saw the priest at the far end of the church. She wanted to bolt but her feet felt stuck to the floor. Now she would catch it. Surely the priest would tell Papa about her disobedience — and who knows what the punishment would be. She shouldn't ever have left the moonlit room and the safe sound of Wolfi's steady breathing.

The priest started walking down the aisle towards her! She forced herself to her feet and ran as fast as she could — down, down, down the steps. She pushed at the door. It wouldn't budge. She couldn't let the priest see her! She pushed again, this time throwing her weight against it. She stumbled onto the street and ran across it and up the steps of the inn. She stood outside their room for a minute, her heart pounding, and suddenly she didn't care about the priest or Papa. The feel of the keys under her fingers and the pedals under her feet had made up for any punishment she would get. She opened the door, took off her dress and cape, and lay down beside Wolfi. Her heart slowed down, and before she knew it, Nannerl was asleep.

Papa frowned as he met them the next day on the steps of the blacksmith shop. "Now they're fixing the other wheel," he said irritably. "Who knows what the cost of all this will be, since I must provide for the driver and the horses as long as we are here and until we get to Munich. I must write Herr Hagenauer for more money."

As they walked back to the inn, the priest walked towards them importantly, holding something in his hand. As he came closer, Nannerl saw that it was Salome Musch. She felt her stomach turn over. How could she have forgotten Salome? Now the priest would tell everything and she would be found out. Papa would be furi-ous, Mama's lips would tighten and Wolfi would smirk a little, as if she were some grand joke. She kicked the toe of her shoe into a crack between two cobblestones. She wanted to run away.

"Good morning, Father," said Papa.

"Good morning, Herr Mozart, Frau Mozart," said the priest. He turned to Wolfi and smiled, then held the doll out in front of him. Nannerl sucked in her breath and then looked down, clenching a bit of skirt in her fist. "I want to thank you for last night's concert," he said to Wolfi with a wink. "It was most splendid. I think you forgot something." He handed Salome over to Wolfi, who stared at the priest as if he were crazy.

Nannerl let out a long breath of relief. Mama and Papa just smiled and nodded.

"Say thank you, Wolfgang," whispered Mama, push-ing him towards the priest.

"Thank you," said Wolfi, looking puzzled. Nannerl smiled. She couldn't believe her luck.

"You are most welcome. Good day," said the priest, and with a little bow, walked away down the street.

"But I didn't have Salome Musch yesterday after-noon," said Wolfi, looking at the doll in his hands. "How could I forget something that wasn't even there?"

Nannerl felt her heart thumping again. She couldn't

lie. But what could she say to make Wolfi stop asking questions?

"I had Salome. I must have forgotten her on a shelf of the organ. I'm sorry, Wolfi. From now on it should just be you who takes care of Salome — I'm too old for her anyway," she said, and skipped ahead to the inn.

After lunch, when everyone else was resting in the room out of the noonday heat, Nannerl got out her diary.

June 10, 1763

Dear Diary,

I will never forget the sound of the great organ, how it washed all over me like a thunderstorm while I played. It was worth all the scariness.

And the priest and Wolfi and Mama and Papa will never know — it's a secret for the moon and me. I think I'll put an organ part in my symphony — now that I know more about how it works. Papa says we'll probably be in Wasserburg for another day, for the other wheel to get fixed. He's very angry.

Love, Nannerl

~ 6 ~

THE NYMPHENBURG CONCERT

NANNERL TRIED TO PLACE two flowers across the rim of her bonnet, but she just couldn't get them to swoop stylishly above her eyes in the way that Katherl had described. They would either fall off or hang way down over her face. She looked in the mirror and threw the flowers onto the floor. Wolfi picked them up and stuck them behind his ear.

"C'mon, Nannerl. Papa says we have to get in the carriage and go. Don't worry about a few silly flowers," he said. "I'll race you down the stairs."

Nannerl followed but she didn't race. After all, this was the big city of Munich, capital of Bavaria, not just an unimportant little town like Wasserburg. Last night, as soon as their carriage had passed under the Isar Gate, she'd looked over at the distant buildings she knew belonged to Nymphenburg Palace, the residence of the Elector, ruler of the whole state of Bavaria!

Now she walked slowly, staring at all the rich ladies who chattered and fanned themselves in the lobby. She swished her skirts the way they did, pretending she was nineteen. She sneaked glances at her reflection in the mirrors that lined the walls. This was the fanciest hotel in Munich. Papa always made sure they stayed at the best hotels, so he could meet important people and get invitations for her and Wolfi to perform.

She stepped outside, squinting and adjusting her bonnet. The carriage was waiting for her, just as if she were a real rich lady! Wolfi stuck his head out the window.

"Hurry up, Fraulein Mozart, or you'll miss the carriage to Nymphenburg!" he said, crossing his eyes. Nannerl forgot that she was supposed to be nineteen and ran to the carriage. Today was the Feast of St Anthony, and the Mozarts were celebrating the holiday with a trip to the four castles and gardens of Nymphenburg Palace, which stood just on the outskirts of Munich. Nannerl had performed there before. She could hardly wait to walk along the canal and see all the people in their fancy boats. And the last time there had been rows and rows of lilac trees in full bloom! She closed her eyes and tried to remember the smell, how she'd buried her face in the purple blossoms.

The carriage bumped over a bridge and Nannerl looked down at the Isar River and all the boats. This wouldn't just be a holiday. Papa was hoping to get an invitation for her and Wolfi to perform before Maximilian the Third, the great Elector of Bavaria.

Nannerl sighed and crossed her arms. She knew they needed the money, but someday it would be nice just to go somewhere and not have to try to impress people for invitations to play. You had to be so careful not to offend the rulers in any way, or they might not ask you to play, or might not give very much for your concert. All the same, she could hardly wait for the carriage ride to be over.

She had been ten when they'd last played for the Elector. After the concert, he had taken her aside. He hadn't looked like a great Elector — short, shrivelled and thin, with eyes the colour of dark coffee and a very long nose. "Your music hit me here," he'd told her, tapping his chest. "Never stop playing, my dear, never stop playing. Even though I rule all of Bavaria, I still compose music and play the violoncello." His voice had sounded like a cello — thick and rich — it seemed much bigger than he was. Now Nannerl wanted to play for him again, to hear that voice and weave it into her symphony.

"Papa, can we see the Badenburg castle and the Amalienburg castle this time?" Wolfi asked, as the carriage rolled down the long driveway to the gardens.

"If we have time," said Papa with his squirmy smile. "First we must all take a little stroll around the gardens."

Nannerl groaned inside. She always hated that part, showing off so that the rulers and important people would know they had arrived. Taking a little stroll meant they would have to promenade right down the great walk in front of Nymphenburg Palace.

"Nannerl, let me fix your bonnet," said Mama, as they stepped out of the carriage. Nannerl let Mama smooth a few wrinkles in her dress and bonnet, then grabbed Wolfi's hand and raced off to look at one of the white marble statues. Mama and Papa came after them.

"I will have none of this racing around," said Papa. "We must walk, very slowly, under the great window."

Nannerl blushed and looked down. Everyone must be watching them, thinking they were silly. She wished she could hide out somewhere in the woods, away from all the eyes that must be noticing her bonnet, how it wouldn't stay on straight.

"Look, Papa, someone wants to see us," said Wolfi, pointing to a tall man hurrying towards them.

"Herr Mozart! Frau Mozart!" he said. "I am Herr Zweibrücken, an assistant to the Elector." He gave Papa a small bow. "What a wonderful surprise! When did you arrive in Munich?"

"Last night," said Papa. "We are indeed honoured to visit these gardens and the palace of the Elector. Everyone tells me he's still in good health and playing music as usual."

"Yes, I don't think anything could come between the Elector and his cello. He's up and practising with the birds every morning without fail. Does he know that you are here?"

"No," piped up Wolfi. "Do you think we could play for him?"

Papa looked embarrassed, but the man just laughed. He ordered a servant to ask the Elector. "Enjoy the gardens," he said. "I'll send a message as soon as I know."

They continued down the walk. It wound around a long sloping lawn and down into a huge rose garden. Nannerl bent over to smell a delicate pink rose, her birth flower.

"Look out, Nannerl! A huge bee's heading straight for your ear!" Wolfi was jumping up and down and pointing over her shoulder. She looked carefully in the direction of his finger. No bee. He giggled and she wanted to pinch him, but he ran away and bumped into a footman, who walked towards them with a piece of paper.

Papa took it and cleared his throat. "Maximilian the Third, Elector of Bavaria, would be most pleased if Wolfgang Amadeus and Maria Anna Mozart of Salzburg would perform before the court in the great ballroom of Nymphenburg Palace on Monday, the thirteenth day of June, in the year seventeen hundred and sixty three, at eight o'clock in the evening." He smiled triumphantly and fished out his pocket watch. "Eight o'clock. We have four hours. What's your wish?"

"Amalienburg and Badenburg!" shouted Wolfi and Nannerl.

"Very well," said Papa, and they took the long, winding path that led through the gardens to the castle.

Wolfi and Nannerl skipped ahead. "What are you going to perform?" asked Wolfi. "I think I'm just going to play whatever comes to my head."

Nannerl glanced over and saw how he held his head high and stuck out his chest. She knew he could easily improvise at a concert. He did it all the time, at home. Once she had tried, but Papa had told her to get back to her scales. "Little girls musn't give in to flights of the imagination," he had said, and she had felt that familiar prickle under her fingers, asking why? as they touched the keys.

"I'll probably play the sonata by Johann Christian Bach," she told Wolfi, and then they both stopped and gazed up at Amalienburg, which had at one time been a hunting lodge.

"C'mon, Nannerl, let's look at the great hall of mirrors," said Wolfi, pulling her inside.

The hall was as high as a church, and circular, so that everywhere you looked were mirrors. Huge mirrors covered every inch of space on every wall; oval mirrors with frames made of gold leaves and fruit, mirrors surrounded by twisted gold candlesticks and long mirrors that reached to the ceiling.

Wolfi pulled her on to Badenburg castle, with its famous marble bath. Fountains spilled out of statues and into the warm water that was known to have the powers of healing. Nannerl yawned. The heavy air made her feel sleepy.

As they left, lightning flashed across the sky and Nannerl covered her ears to the thunder and rain that followed.

"Run!" shouted Papa. She and Mama picked up their skirts and ran along the little path after Wolfi and Papa to Nymphenburg Palace. By the time they arrived panting at the back servants' quarters they were completely soaked. Water dripped from Nannerl's bonnet and ran down her face. She slumped into a chair and stared at her mud-splotched dress.

"Now what are we going to do?" she wailed, pulling at her wet wig. "How can we play for the Elector in these messy clothes!" She squeezed water from her bonnet and threw it down onto a puddle.

"Nannerl!" Mama said. "Throwing clothes won't help." Then she smiled and pointed to a small trunk. Wolfi ran over to it and pulled out dry clothes and wigs. Mama must have slipped it in here on the way to the castles! Nannerl ran over to where Mama stood. "Thank you," she said, giving her a wet hug.

"Never mind," Mama said, hugging Nannerl back

and then bustling by the fire. "There's still lots to do before the concert." Soon their wet clothes dried by the fire while Mama helped Wolfi into his dry vest and little coat and knickers. Nannerl hoped that Mama had packed her lucky performance dress, but she pulled out her second favourite instead, the purple one with the big crinoline. She got Mama to lace her corset really tight. She didn't care if it felt awful. Tonight she must look perfect.

Mama passed around bread and fruit and cheese and Nannerl took more than Wolfi; running through the storm had made her hungry. Then a footman came to tell them the Elector was ready, and they followed Papa to the ballroom door.

Nannerl peeked around the corner. Ladies in rustling silk gowns sat at tables sipping tea and nibbling chocolates. Gentlemen stood in little groups in the corners. And there was the Elector, sitting in a huge chair with two sleeping dogs at his feet! He looked just as Nannerl remembered him — so small and thin — he seemed to be swallowed up by his chair. But his voice was the opposite of his appearance. Nannerl caught it sliding above the chatter, warm and full as a pot of thick soup. All she wanted now was to sit down at the clavier and play for him.

A hush fell as the Mozart family entered and sat in the chairs beside the clavier.

Papa bowed to a smattering of applause. "I will let

the music make the introductions. Ladies and gentlemen of the court ... my son, Wolfgang Amadeus Mozart." Wolfi gave a little bow, and the ladies whispered *Wunderkind* and clucked their tongues as he sat down at the clavier. Nannerl closed her eyes and felt the knots in her stomach loosen as Wolfi played. She smiled. He was improvising.

First, he played a simple and direct theme. Then he started on the variations, each one growing a little more difficult, but always keeping some important part of the tune. Nannerl played games like trying to guess how he would change each variation. So far she had guessed five out of seven correctly. Then she guessed how many variations in total he would play. Ten? No, he was playing another one. Twelve? Thirteen? Yes, thirteen, because today was June 13.

She glanced anxiously at the clock on the wall. Wolfi had been playing for over an hour. She wished he would stop, then scolded herself for the thought. Wolfi should play as long as he wanted and it was fun to listen to him ... but ... well, soon he would be finished and then she would play. She looked at the Elector, sitting forward in his chair, his dark eyes glued to Wolfi. Her hands felt cold and clammy. She wiggled her fingers to warm them up. Soon ... soon it would be her turn.

Wolfi finished with a flourish and stood up to bow.

Thirteen variations! The applause sounded like the afternoon's thunderstorm. Nannerl got ready to stand and curtsy. Surely they would stop clapping for Wolfi soon! But they wouldn't stop, not until he had bowed and got out his violin. Papa sat at the clavier. Nannerl sat back and groaned inside. Now Wolfi and Papa would play a concerto for violin and clavier — and it was already almost nine-thirty!

This time, instead of listening to Wolfi, she went through the sonata in her head, planning exactly how she would play each phrase to make the Elector lean forward and smile, enjoy her performance just as much as he seemed to be liking Wolfi's. She rubbed her fingers and flexed them and rubbed them again. Finally, the applause rang through the hall. Now she would play.

But Herr Zweibrücken, the man they'd met that afternoon, was walking to the clavier! He introduced two women, a baroness and a countess from Vienna. They came forward, smiling and curtsying. There was a small applause. Nannerl counted the number of buttons on the back of Mama's dress. "These distinguished ladies both wish to honour the court and the Elector with a few songs," said Herr Zweibrücken. "First ... Madame Baroness."

Her voice was warbly, always shaking and on the verge of collapse, like the gelatin Mama sometimes made on summer afternoons. It finally burst, squawking on the high C like an old crow. Nannerl shivered and looked at the clock. Twenty-five to eleven! Would they never finish? The Countess was easier to listen to, although at times she sounded like the rusty scrape of the carriage door. Nannerl yawned and felt her eyelids droop, then sat forward in her chair. She musn't sleep. Surely they would still let her play! She saw the ladies at the tables politely covering yawns with their lace handkerchiefs. The Countess finished. Nannerl rose to play. But others were beginning to stand and gather their cloaks!

It was a quarter to eleven. People wanted to go home. Nannerl sank into her chair. She felt numb. She wanted to sleep, but also she wanted to punch the Baroness with the quavery gelatin voice and the big bosom. She wanted to punch Wolfi for making up so many variations. She wanted to punch the people for making him play again. The Elector ... where was the Elector? She saw him link arms with two women and walk out of the room.

Mama squeezed her hand and almost carried her to the carriage. The ache was lodged in Nannerl's throat as if it meant to stay there, always, a reminder of this horrible concert where she was not allowed to play. She couldn't cry. All the way back into the city she pretended to sleep, shivering and hunched in the corner against the cold window.

It was a quarter past eleven when they reached the

room at the inn. Nannerl went straight to her bed. At least she had one to herself this time, and a little partition so that it was almost like having a room of her own. She lit a candle and got out her diary. She had to write. It was the only way to get rid of the ache.

June 13, 1763

Dear Diary,

This was the worst night of my life. They didn't let me play for the Elector. I want to pound pound pound on the clavier until all the strings break and I want to throw Wolfi's violin in the fire. I'm just not going to play these concerts any more. That will show them. I want to run away, back to my friends in Salzburg who like me. Katherl — why has she not sent any letters with Herr Hagenauer? I've already sent one with Papa. Has she forgotten about me, so soon? I can still remember her laugh and her loud voice, the way she kneels and uses fancy language like an actor. She was going to help me with my symphony — I might as well throw that in the fire too. I'm trying to write the organ part and it seems impossible. I feel stupid and ugly and I hate the Baroness. Goodbye.

Maria Anna Walburga Ignatia Mozart

Nannerl blew out the candle and dug her fingers into the sheets. Writing had helped a bit. The ache softened and finally came out of her throat in sobs. Gigantic sobs, the kind that made her whole body shake but also comforted, somehow. And then she felt a strong hand on her back moving over and over, in circles, in rhythm to her sobs. "Sh, Nannerl, sh," Mama whispered and stroked her hair with strong fingers, over and over, until the sobs were quiet and Nannerl was asleep with Mama's arms around her.

❧ 7 ❧

⌀OPHERL

"⌀ WISH THE ELECTOR would hurry and pay us," said Papa. "Wolfi gave the most splendid concert on Monday night, and now it is already Saturday. We are scheduled to leave Munich and travel on, but we can't without our much deserved money! It is really most exasperating." He stood up. "Perhaps today, at his lunch in town, the Elector will finally give us the money we need to pay for all of this!" He swept his arm around the room.

"Come, children, hurry and get ready," Papa continued. "If we arrive early enough, we might even have the good fortune to sit at the Elector's table."

Nannerl dawdled over to the wardrobe. Mention of the Elector made her ache again as she had on Monday after the concert. She looked at her dresses. Who cared what she wore? She never wanted to speak to the Elector again, anyway. She chose her ugliest dress, the yellow one she had had since she was ten.

But she wished she had worn something nicer when they reached the grand house on Augusten Street. It looked like a palace. She and Wolfi strolled through the gardens beside fountains and flowers and around hedges trimmed to look like birds and animals. And inside! Nannerl had to hold Wolfi's hand tight to keep him from running around the tables and grabbing food.

She had never seen such a feast; steaming platters of trout and chicken; tureens of soup and bowls of green asparagus, not the white kind they ate at home; platters piled high with melons, figs, grapes, apples and pears; dishes with funny looking noodles covered in crumbly cheese; boiled eggs cut open with stuffing inside, and cakes ... cakes of every shape and colour, cakes covered with cream and with chocolate, cakes with strawberries dipped in pudding, and *Gugelhupf* cakes as high as Mama's wig!

Wolfi and Nannerl stood and stared, until Papa came up behind them and guided them over to the table where the Elector sat.

"I am honoured to sit with the *Wunderkindern* from Salzburg," said the Elector with a smile. Nannerl looked at her hands and remembered the concert. She wished they didn't have to sit with him.

"Master Wolfgang, I was most amazed at your performance the other night. I, too, am a composer, but never would have thought it possible to improvise thirteen variations on a single theme! And in a concert!"

"And I have met you before, in your beautiful music." Nannerl looked up quickly and saw the Elector's dark eyes smiling straight at her. He suddenly looked so small, lost in his big chair, with all the people clustered around him. He was like Wolfi — you couldn't be mad at him for long. "That meeting I shall never forget," he continued. "I was very sorry not to have heard you the other night." He glanced over at Papa.

The Elector was on her side! He hadn't forgotten about her after all! Nannerl felt a tingling in her fingers and stabbed a strawberry triumphantly with her fork.

"This is my sister, Frau Maria Sophia, from Paris," continued the Elector, turning to the woman beside him. "We call her Sopherl. Sopherl, meet Herr and Frau Mozart, and their two children, Wolfgang and Nannerl."

Nannerl couldn't help staring at Sopherl. She was much older than Mama, and not nearly as handsome. Her face looked pinched and pale, as if she'd been shut up in quiet rooms for a long time without fresh air. She didn't smile but she wasn't mean-looking either — her mouth stayed in a steady line that sometimes twitched ever so slightly but never opened to talk. Her silence was like those big pauses in a symphony, when all the notes and chattery scales that have been building up for so long stop suddenly — the quiet before a big thunderstorm, when the air is dark and full and you listen harder than ever because you don't know what might burst from it.

Sopherl looked up from her plate to sip some wine and Nannerl caught a glimpse of her eyes. They were dark as her silence and held secrets, sad secrets from a time that had long ago passed.

"... and do you still play the violoncello, Elector?" Papa was asking as he lifted a forkful of steaming trout.

"Every night and every morning. I have never stopped playing. It has been a part of my life since I was a small boy. Sopherl and I used to have wonderful evenings of music at Nymphenburg." He looked at his sister and she seemed almost to smile.

Sopherl had played music! Nannerl felt questions boiling inside her. One popped to the surface before she could stop it. "Sopherl, what instrument did you play?"

"Sh, Nannerl," said Papa. She saw his flushed face and felt like crawling under the table. Someone whispered something about girls not knowing how to hold their tongues any more, and didn't she know the Elector's sister never spoke in public?

But Sopherl's mouth was partly open and she looked as if she might answer. Nannerl leaned forward in her chair, her heart thumping — maybe now Sopherl's voice would break the pause and unravel her secrets.

"My sister ..." the Elector awkwardly cleared his voice, "doesn't speak much outside of the family. But I can assure you, Nannerl, that she once played very well indeed." He bent his head, intent on slicing his trout.

Then people resumed their chatter and Nannerl sat back in her chair and sighed. She wanted to tell the older woman that she hadn't meant to embarrass her, that the question had just slipped out without permission. But Sopherl was looking the other way listening to some ladies discuss the weather, her left hand clenched in a tight fist on the table.

Nannerl heard Papa whispering to Wolfi. "... and tell him we are departing early tomorrow morning!"

Wolfi kneeled on his chair to make himself higher. He cleared his throat. "Elector, do you realize that we are leaving very early tomorrow?" There was a small ripple of laughter. The Elector looked straight at Papa, not smiling. "I should have liked to have heard your little girl," he said quietly.

An uncomfortable silence followed. Papa smiled, but it didn't look as if he meant it. "Well, well, I suppose it does not matter too much if we stay on a few days longer, so Nannerl can play for you," he said pleasantly. "When can we bring her to Nymphenburg Palace?"

The Elector scratched his head. "Hmmm ... let's see. On Monday there is hunting, and on Tuesday a French play. So, Wednesday. Yes, you may come to the palace on Wednesday morning, and I shall hear Nannerl play." He looked at her and smiled.

Nannerl wanted to jump as high as the chandelier and swing on it until she was dizzy, then slip out the high window and fly through the sky for a while. The Elector wanted to hear her play, he wanted to hear *her*! She didn't even mind that he had called her a little girl! She would show them! She would play until her fingers dropped off and then she would play some more. She couldn't stay at this table any longer. She had to run!

"Mama, can Wolfi and I please be excused, to play outside?" Nannerl asked.

"Yes, but be careful of your dress," said Mama.

"Hooray!" shouted Wolfi, hopping down from his chair. As they left, Nannerl turned and looked once more at Sopherl. She was looking back! Her mouth was straight, her eyes were still secret and sad, but her left fist — it was slowly opening, the long white fingers like petals curled slightly inward, as if Sopherl were offering a gift or beckoning her to come over. The shape of Sopherl's hand reminded Nannerl of something and she couldn't figure out what. She stood there puzzling over it until Wolfi grabbed her own hand and pulled her outside.

They danced in circles, around and around until they were both out of breath and fell down onto the grass. Nannerl moved up to the little bench, thinking about her dress. It was an ugly old thing, but she didn't want to worry Mama with grass stains.

"Wolfi, isn't it exciting about the Elector? I want to sing and fly like those birds on that fountain."

"I've been listening to them," said Wolfi. "They make their own songs, without any silly papers or notes. Listen ... they sing them as they fly. I'm going to fly too."

He jumped up on the bench, took a leap with his arms spread out and crashed onto the grass.

Nannerl giggled. "Oh, Wolfi," she said and slipped off the bench to sit down beside him. Nannerl smelled roses as she sat with Wolfi on the grass. Then Mama called for them to leave.

Later that day, she took out her diary.

June 18, 1763

Dear Diary,

I will play at Nymphenburg after all! The Elector looked right at Papa, almost glaring, and told him he was sorry not to have heard me! I am carefully planning everything. I will wear my special good luck performance dress — not just a travel dress, as Mama wished, since we are to leave right after the concert. (After Papa pays the owner of this inn!) The only thing missing is what to play. I want to play something extra, something special, just for

the Elector. I keep thinking about Sopherl, and
wishing I could hear her voice.

Love, Nannerl

Over the next few days, during the sightseeing excursions and meals at the inn, all the clavier pieces Nannerl knew kept running through her head as she tried to decide what to play. She was still thinking about it on Wednesday as she waited in the servants' quarters at Nymphenburg. She would start with the Johann Christian Bach sonata. After that ... well, maybe for once she would stop always trying to make plans and just do what she felt. Papa was off somewhere, arranging a carriage for the next stage of the journey. She felt oddly calm, fingering the lace of her lucky performance dress. Her hands weren't even clammy as she and Mama and Wolfi followed the footman to the ballroom.

Morning sunlight streamed in through the huge windows. Several ladies were seated at tables drinking tea. There in his big chair was the Elector, smiling and pressing his fingers together. Nannerl curtsied and sat down at the clavier.

She began the sonata the way she had planned. Slowly, as if she were walking through a dark forest with gigantic old trees. With every phrase she stroked an old tree trunk in a different way, feeling the rough bark. Then she came out into the open meadow, and the music was fast as she skipped and danced with the butterflies. Then came that long trill, the one she had practised every morning for months in Salzburg until it was perfect. The time came to move onto the next section, but ... what was happening? Were her right fingers stuck? She couldn't leave the trill. It was as if her fingers were playing without her.

Then she heard the birds in the meadow. They wanted to trill the whole day and they didn't care who heard them. Suddenly she felt like laughing. Her left hand started to play its own melody to go along with the trilling birds and soon everybody in the forest was following Nannerl's left hand melody out of the meadow and onto a winding path through the high grass. It was full of unexpected turns. By the time she reached a lake, Nannerl was hot and dived into the water with all her clothes on — splash!

There was silence in the great ballroom. She looked at her hands, trembling above the keys. Her forehead was wet with sweat that trickled down to her nose. She felt weak, but it was a good kind of weak, as if she had just finished a race with Wolfi. She stood up in a kind of daze and curtsied. Nannerl didn't dare look at the audience or the Elector, and followed Wolfi and Mama out of the room.

She wasn't sure what she had done, whether to cry or

dance. She looked at Wolfi. He was staring at her with wide eyes. "Nannerl, you sure gave old Johann Christian Bach a new turn! I didn't think that trill would ever stop!" he said. "Wait till I tell Papa how magnificent you were!"

"Wolfi, please don't tell Papa. Please?" begged Nannerl, trying to grab him as he ran off.

"Tell Papa what?" Nannerl heard the Elector's cello voice coming up from behind. She turned around and he kneeled and took her hands. "How can I ever thank you for that wonderful gift? It reminded me of music played by my sister — many years ago. She took a similar risk, once," he said. He looked at the floor for a moment, then looked up. "Nannerl, do you remember Sopherl, my sister, from the dinner?"

"Yes. Why?" asked Nannerl. Sopherl. Her silence and strange, sad eyes. The left hand opening towards her.

"She was here today, and heard you play and was very moved by your music. She asked me to tell you how much she enjoyed the concert ... she even said she wished she might see you again."

Nannerl felt something warm leap inside her throat. Sopherl had been in the audience, had walked with her through the forest and the high grass. And now she wanted to see her, not Wolfi or Mama or Papa, but her!

"I've been thinking," continued the Elector. "Your family will be stopping in Paris in December, yes? Your

Papa hopes to get an invitation to play for the King and Queen at the Palace of Versailles?"

"Yes," said Nannerl.

"Sopherl lives in Paris. I can feel it, way down somewhere in my bones, that you and she can help each other and will need each other. Sopherl has not had an easy time ... will you visit her when you're there?"

"But why is Sopherl unhappy?" Nannerl asked.

"Poor Sopherl ... it's, it's not something a child would be able to understand ... " said the Elector. "But please believe me, Sopherl would be happy to see you. Please, see my sister."

Nannerl nodded solemnly.

"I knew you would understand," he said, handing her the carefully written address. Then he took out a small velvet bag with a little gold drawstring, and placed it in her palm. It felt heavy and she almost dropped it.

"Please deliver that to your Papa," he said. "Nannerl, will you promise to come and play for me again?"

"I promise," she said, curtsying and turning to leave.

"Please don't forget about Sopherl!" he called after her.

"Never!" she called back.

The coins in the little bag jingled as she ran.

~§ 8 §~

THE MANNHEIM ORCHESTRA

NANNERL UNFOLDED THE PIECE of paper she had hidden in her diary and traced her finger along the outline of the Elector's writing.

Frau Maria Sophia Wenzel
No. 68 rue François
Paris, France

How would she ever find Sopherl? She would have to ask Mama and Papa for help ... unless she could sneak off at night and find the address! She remembered Wasserburg and smiled to herself. But Paris? Nannerl shivered. It was about fifty times as big as Wasserburg!

"Nannerl, can I write in your diary?" asked Wolfi, rubbing his eyes and stretching. He had been sleeping on her shoulder as the carriage bumped along.

Nannerl crushed the address into her fist and closed her diary. She took a deep breath. "Wolfi," she said, trying to sound patient and calm. Papa was watching them with his squirmy smile. "It was my birthday present, remember? Would you like it if I used ... your violin? Would you?"

"No, but that's not a real example, because you can't play violin anyway," said Wolfi, squirming in the seat and scratching his arm. Nannerl turned and looked at a passing vineyard.

"Come, come, children," said Papa. "The carriage is small enough without quarrels. Nannerl, what would be the harm in Wolfi writing a few lines? There are plenty of pages! And it would be a good educational experience for him to write some of his observations, as you are doing."

"But it's mine ... the things I write are — "

"That's enough, Nannerl," interrupted Papa in a low voice. "You will share it with Wolfi and that's that."

Mama's mouth was set in a straight line — it didn't look as if she would come to the rescue. Nannerl couldn't let go of the diary. She gripped one of the pages, hard, as if she might tear it out and throw it onto the floor of the carriage.

Papa cleared his throat, a warning signal, but before he could get really angry Nannerl flipped to the very last page and slapped the book into Wolfi's hand. She folded her arms and jerked her head towards the window. She wouldn't cry, she wouldn't. But she kept thinking about her birthday party ... Papa lighting her candle ... the new diary and the way they'd all gathered around her. She pulled herself in closer to the window. If only she could kick this carriage open and run away from them, far out into the yellow fields and hills.

Wolfi was wiggling with excitement. "I'm going to write in the language of the country we visit," he announced. "Now I'll write in German, but when we get to the Netherlands — Dutch, and in Paris — French."

Nannerl tightened her arms against her chest. That had been her idea, hers! She just hadn't told everyone, like Wolfi. No one must see what she had written! From now on, whenever Wolfi used her diary, she would watch very closely. As soon as he was finished, she would take it back. Not fair. She unfolded her arms and scratched the words into a fold of her dress. *Not fair.*

"Are we almost in Ludwigsburg?" Mama asked. "I do hope the Duke will give us an invitation to play."

Papa frowned and turned a few pages in his book. "There's talk that Herr Jommelli, his Italian music director, doesn't think much of Germans. Well, once he hears about Wolfi I'm sure that will change."

Nannerl turned from the window and shifted in her seat. What was Katherl doing right now? Practising the clavier? She wished she had her own clavier! She had finally figured out the organ part for her symphony, but she wanted to hear it played, even if it wasn't on the real organ.

They came to a stop in front of a small toll house. Nannerl took her diary from Wolfi and motioned for him to follow her out of the carriage. She looked to make sure that no one was listening. "Wolfi, you must promise never, ever to read this part of the diary." She took the pages she had written between her thumb and index finger. "You can use the back, but that's it. Please promise."

"Of course, silly," he said, looking at her with his wide blue eyes. But behind his gaze, Nannerl saw mischief. She would have to watch the diary like a cat. She tucked it in her pocket and raced over to watch Papa give the money for the toll.

It was almost dark when they finally reached the Ludwigsburg inn. She woke up early the next morning and saw Papa reading a letter. She quickly got out of bed and dressed. "Papa," she whispered, "Is it from Herr Hagenauer? Is there anything for me?"

Papa shook his head.

"I was hoping for something from Katherl. I still haven't heard from her." Nannerl sighed as she took the chair beside Papa. "Maybe she's forgotten about me."

"I doubt that, Nannerl." He finished reading the letter, then put it in his pocket and turned to her. "How would you like to go shopping with me, right now, before Mama and Wolfi wake up? There's something very special that I want to buy."

"Of course, Papa." Nannerl ran to get her cape. "What is it?"

"It's a secret." He took her hand and together they went out into the quiet morning. Nannerl looked at her feet as she walked. She wasn't quite sure what to say to Papa. It seemed like such a long time since she had been alone with him. Unless you counted that morning back in Salzburg when Wolfi had interrupted.

"When I was a boy, we used to come to this town for concerts at the summer palace," said Papa.

"Did you play?"

"No," said Papa. "We were lucky if we got to sit in the back row. Now look at us — you and Wolfi might even play for the King and Queen of France!"

They reached a bake shop and Papa bought two sticky sweet rolls for them to eat as they walked. Nannerl licked the icing from her fingers as she walked up the street, wishing that the morning would never end.

Papa stopped in front of a store. The fine script on the sign read, *Andreas Stein — Maker of Fine Organs and Claviers*. Papa smiled and opened the door.

A short man with thin grey hair sat behind the counter. "Nannerl, this is Herr Stein," said Papa. "He is famous throughout Europe for his craft."

The little man blushed and smiled. "So, Herr Mozart, you have come for the — "

"Sh!" said Papa, smiling. "Can you lead us to it?"

Nannerl's heart raced as she followed Papa and Herr Stein to the back room. A clavier stood alone in the middle of the room, small and fragile, with thin, spindly legs, like a colt. Nannerl ran her hand along the smooth wood. "Papa, is it for us?"

Papa smiled and nodded. "Herr Stein has built it small enough to bring with us on our travels. Now you and Wolfi have no excuse not to practise! Why don't you try it?"

She sat down at the little instrument and began to play. She stroked the new keys over and over, not able to get enough of their smooth feel. She, not Wolfi, was the first to play it. Her symphony — she would be able to play the parts now, when everybody else was away, of course, but still — she knew she could finish it now, in time for Johann Christian Bach.

But how would Papa pay for the clavier? He was always complaining about not having enough money. She stopped playing as Papa opened the Elector's small velvet bag with the little gold drawstring. As he and Herr Stein began to count out the coins, she remembered the address in Paris the Elector had given to her along with the money. She turned back to the small instrument and played faster and harder, her head filling with plans.

July 11, 1763

Dear Diary,

Wolfi has been playing on the new clavier for the last two hours and he won't stop, even though I begged to have some practise time. And Papa won't stop him, just sits and writes a letter to Herr Hagenauer.

Papa is in a terrible humour, too. Wolfi and I weren't invited to play for the Duke after all. Papa says that Herr Jommelli, the Duke's Italian music director, doesn't believe that a German child like Wolfi can be a genius.

But now, even though we can't play, we have to stay here in Ludwigsburg because the Duke took all the post horses and hired coachmen for a hunting trip. Papa has tried to round up some horses, but it looks like we're stuck here for another day. There are soldiers everywhere in this town. Outside I can hear their drums and shouts, and the sound of their feet as they march.

Papa says that we might see the famous

Mannheim orchestra — I can hardly wait to hear the horns and the flutes.

Wolfi is still playing. If only I could practise early, like I did in Salzburg. But I'd wake everyone in this small room. But I have a plan — tonight, when everybody else goes for the after-supper walk, I'll say I'd rather practise and I'll stay up here and work on my symphony.

Goodbye. Nannerl

That evening, as soon as the others were safely on their walk, Nannerl took out Wolfi's violin and practised a bit. She'd done this a few times in Salzburg, but now on the tour it was hard to find a time when he wasn't around. She tried to hold the bow the way she'd seen Wolfi do so many times, then experimented with a few notes.

After a few minutes she put the violin away and played the flute melody of her symphony on the little clavier. She frowned and scribbled out a note, put the quill pen down and played the line again. It sounded tight. Something was holding it back, like the corset squeezing her chest when she tried to outrun Wolfi. She closed her eyes and tried to remember the sound of the flute in the Salzburg orchestra, but instead she heard

Katherl's big voice when it filled a room and the way the birds had trilled in the garden at the Elector's dinner. She grabbed the pen and scribbled again, giving the flute a long, high trill and marking it *forte*. She smiled. Now the melody was winding easily around in her head and she just had to write fast enough to get it on the page.

The clock in the Ludwigsburg town square struck seven times and Nannerl wrote faster. She wanted to play the finished flute part on the clavier before Mama and Papa and Wolfi came back. Her fingers began to ache as they translated the sound from her head into notes. There — she sketched the last half note with a flourish, propped the sheets of music on the ledge of the clavier and began to play, listening closely to the flute melody and imagining the other instruments that would play at the same time.

Wolfi suddenly burst into the room and Nannerl whisked the music under her crinoline; at least the scratchy petticoat was good for something. She started to play a difficult sonata by Johann Gottfried Eckhardt.

"Papa found some horses after all!" Wolfi interrupted her practice and came over to the clavier. "We're leaving tomorrow for Schwetzingen, the summer palace of Karl Theodor! Papa's arranged a concert for us there, and the famous Mannheim orchestra will play in the same concert!"

Papa smiled as he entered the room; he was in a good mood again. Mama pulled out the trunks and began to pack, then looked over at Nannerl.

"Are you feeling all right, Nannerl? You look a little pale. Too bad you couldn't join us for our walk," she said.

"I'm fine, Mama," said Nannerl, fishing out the sheets of music from under her crinoline and shoving them into the book of sonatas by Eckhardt.

"Then you can pack your and Wolfi's clothing trunks and help me with the bedding and the candles," said Mama in a tired voice.

"Yes, Mama," said Nannerl. Wolfi began to play. It didn't seem fair that she had to pack his trunk while he got to practise. She opened her wardrobe and saw her performance dress glowing rose in the dim evening light. She drew her finger over the satin, humming the tune of the flute.

She was still humming it in her head the next day in the carriage as they drove to Schwetzingen. The summer palace was supposed to have beautiful gardens and woods, like Nymphenburg. Her heart beat harder when she thought about hearing the famous Mannheim orchestra.

"I remember the players," Papa said as they bumped along. "They are neither drinkers, nor gamblers, nor rascals. Both their conduct and their playing are most virtuous. And I shall never forget the famous flautist, Johann

Baptist Wendling. I hear he is making quite a career of his brilliant flute playing, with frequent engagements in London and Paris."

"Papa, could I play the flute please?" asked Wolfi, craning his neck to look out the window. "I'd like to write some music for it. Maybe I could try Herr Wendling's instrument?"

"A splendid idea, Wolfi," Papa nodded. "I'm sure he'd be thrilled to give you some instruction after the concert."

The flute melody that had been running through Nannerl's head all day clenched up like a fist. Somehow, it didn't seem like hers any more. She had to find a place to unwind it, somehow, hear it playing as it had before. She was suddenly so tired of the faces of Mama and Papa and Wolfi. She wanted to be alone. But as soon as they reached the country inn on the outskirts of the Schwetzingen Palace, Wolfi grabbed her hand.

"Race me to the fountain?"

Nannerl shook her head.

"C'mon, Nannerl. We've been cooped up in the carriage all day. Let's explore!" He swept his arm around to the gardens, the palace off in the distance, the long driveway with its rows of trees.

"Sorry, Wolfi. I'll join you later." Nannerl turned away and ran towards the inn. She went straight up to their room and dug through her trunk for her symphony, found the flute part and started to hum it, quiet enough so that Mama and Sebastian, unloading trunks, wouldn't hear. She glanced out the window and saw Wolfi slowly making figure-eights around the trees, his head down, his hands in his pockets. Part of her wanted to go outside, take his hand and explore, but she stayed right where she was.

In the days that followed, Nannerl made a count-down to the concert on a little calendar she had made in her diary, imagining the sound of the flute. And she snatched all the time she could at the clavier, practising extra hard. She wanted to play the Eckhardt sonata perfectly. Papa had said it was one of the most difficult works ever written. Well, it was the hardest thing she had ever played. One day she drilled the sixteenth note passage on the second page for four hours!

Finally, the day of the concert came. The performance was to begin at five o'clock in the afternoon, to allow plenty of time for the Mannheim orchestra. Nannerl stepped from the carriage at the palace and remembered the concert at Nymphenburg. What if they ran out of time and she wasn't allowed to play?

They stepped inside and Nannerl heard the sound of clarinets and violins warming up in some distant room of the palace. She stopped and listened for the flute ... yes, there it was, its clear sound rising above the other instruments.

The music director of the court stood at the front. He twisted his hands and frowned, scanning his list for an opening performance. He looked up and Nannerl felt his gaze. Her hands tingled. The director cleared his throat.

"Yes, well, on tonight's gala concert, we are pleased to have with us a most unusually gifted pair of children — Wolfgang Amadeus and Maria Anna Mozart, from Salzburg. We shall begin with them." He nodded and sat down. Papa cleared his throat and got ready to stand, but Nannerl stood and curtsied before he could say anything. The audience applauded and she looked over at Papa, his mouth open in surprise. She hadn't really meant to jump up like that, but she was so anxious to play — and she was tired of always waiting and having to go second!

It was definitely better, going first. Her hands hadn't had time to go clammy and her mind was clear and uncluttered with the music of Wolfi or anybody else. She was glad she had done all that work on the second page of the Eckhardt sonata. The notes flew out from underneath her fingers like purplish-blue butterflies set free from a cage. The second movement was slower, like the horses when they got tired, or Wolfi's slow footsteps making figure-eights around the trees. The third movement was a quick dance and Nannerl thought of the jumpy marionette puppets in the Salzburg town square on Saturday afternoons.

She sat down, breathless and flushed. Her heart was beating hard and she felt like running around. She wiped her wet hands on the skirt of her dress while the huge applause rang loud and clear in her ears. Papa stood up and gave Wolfi a long-winded introduction, then put a long black cloth over his small hands so he couldn't see the keyboard. Nannerl sighed and listened to Wolfi play.

But they didn't ask him for an encore this time. Everybody was probably too anxious to hear the Mannheim orchestra. Nannerl and Wolfi sat on the edges of their seats while the members of the orchestra came forward and sat down. The concertmaster remained standing and played an A on his violin to help the orchestra tune. Wolfi poked Nannerl in the ribs.

"See Herr Wendling?" he whispered. "He's the skinny bald one with the googly eyes in the second row, behind the violas. I hope he doesn't play like a giraffe, because he looks like one!"

Nannerl stifled a giggle and a hush fell over the audience as the conductor came forward. She looked at the rows of men with their gleaming instruments, poised at the edge of their chairs. They stared at the conductor, and when he gave the cue with his baton, they began to play.

They played like the insides of clocks that Nannerl
had seen at the repair shop; each part fitted to the other,
the wheels and cogs ticking in perfect rhythm, blending
into a whole, huge, sound. They played for two hours but
to Nannerl it seemed like ten minutes. She didn't want
them to stop. She realized suddenly that Katherl had been
right — her symphony was too big. How could she have
thought that she needed so many violins? This orchestra
only had twelve. She tried to memorize the way Herr
Wendling's flute embroidered the string sounds, winding
around the cellos and violins with a tone like silky blue
thread.

When the applause finally died down, Nannerl stayed
stuck to her chair and braced herself for Papa's lecture
about little girls who stood up to play before they were
even introduced. She turned around finally and noticed
with relief that Papa was way at the back of the hall talking to an elderly gentleman. And of course Wolfi was
already up at the front, showing Herr Wendling his little
violin. Nannerl stood up and almost ran over to them.

"... offff courssssse you can try it," Herr Wendling
was saying with a smile. "I'mmmmm honoured to have
such a fine musician play my flute." He showed Wolfi
how to blow.

Nannerl hung back and watched. While Wolfi was
experimenting with the flute, Herr Wendling suddenly

noticed her, walked over, kneeled down and took her hand to kiss it.

"Fffffraulein Mozart, congratulations on an absssssolutely exquisite performance," he stuttered. "Never before, not even in Pppparis or London, have I heard Eckhardt played with such accuracy, with such absolute precision and bbbbrilliance. I was truly moved by your performance."

Nannerl wanted to stare at the floor, but instead she forced herself to look him straight in the eye. "Thank you," she said. "I didn't want the sound of your flute to stop."

"Will you two play at the Christmas Day concert at the Palace of Versailles?" he asked.

"Papa hopes that we will," said Nannerl.

"They will be lucky to hear you," he said. "Now, I really must be going. I have kept my colleagues waiting again, I see. Good evening!"

Papa came over to tell them it was time to go. Now Nannerl braced herself for the lecture. But Papa was wearing a grin.

"Well, dear Nannerl, you certainly caused a sensation with your Eckhardt tonight. I was just talking to an acquaintance of that mean composer Schobert. And apparently, Schobert was in a complete rage of jealousy over your brilliant and precise execution of the difficult piece. He couldn't conceal his jealousy, made quite a laughing stock of himself I hear," Papa chuckled to himself and ruffled her hair. "Well, well, I am very proud of my little girl."

Nannerl glowed with the praise, even though she was getting very tired of people always calling her a little girl. She wished she could be like Wolfi and just say, "Please don't call me a little girl because I'm not one any more." But she couldn't say that to Papa. Not yet.

Nannerl felt like dancing. She took Wolfi's hand and together they skipped out to the carriage, where Mama waited with their capes because the summer night was growing late and cold. She shivered and thought about Paris, Christmas, and the way her flute melody might float above these houses like wisps of smoke. And maybe, in Paris, she would see Sopherl.

𝒲OLFI's ℱEVER 𝒯UNE

"𝒲E SHOULD REACH Coblenz in time for supper," said the captain of the river boat, shielding his eyes as he held the wheel. The Mozarts had set sail down the Rhine River over a week ago, and Nannerl could hardly wait to see Coblenz. Papa had said it was an important port city because two rivers intersected there — the Rhine and the Mosel.

She clutched the wooden rail and looked out at the stormy waves. The cold September wind slapped rain against her face as she peered up at dark castles that rose from the steep, rocky bank, their windows blinking like yellow eyes in the rain. Nannerl loved the wild rhythm of the waves. She wasn't a bit seasick, not like Wolfi and Mama, who had been tossing and turning below for the past three days. The boat kept having to take refuge ashore because of strong winds.

She looked up at the wall of rock and forest, remembering the stories Mama had told her about the Lorelei, the beautiful water nymph of the Rhine who sat combing her long yellow hair. Sailors would see her and be so distracted by her beauty that they would crash into the rocks and die. Nannerl looked down at the foamy waves, trying to catch the shiny flicker of the Lorelei's tail or the glint of her flaxen hair. She began to hum the song that told the story.

"Nannerl, you shouldn't stay out so long in the rain or you'll catch a chill," Papa said as he hoisted himself up from the lower deck. "Wolfi's seasickness is worse than ever, and now he's caught a proper cold as well. It's a good thing we've almost reached Coblenz. Now come down where it's warm, for the rest of the trip."

"But Papa," argued Nannerl. "It's only a short while until Coblenz and I don't feel a bit cold. Besides, the fresh air keeps me from being seasick."

"Well ... maybe just a few minutes longer," relented Papa, coming over to stand beside her and lean out over the railing.

Nannerl smiled. It seemed that ever since that concert at Schwetzingen with the Mannheim orchestra, when she had played the difficult Eckhardt sonata and made that composer Schobert jealous, Papa had acted differently, somehow. At concerts, he had sometimes introduced her first. He seemed to listen to the things she said more often. And he didn't say no as much.

"Are you getting tired of travelling?" asked Papa.

Nannerl thought of Katherl. "I miss Salzburg," she said. "We left in June. Now it's already September and I still haven't heard from Katherl. Every time you open a letter from Herr Hagenauer, I wonder if there'll be something for me from Katherl. But every time there's nothing and I wonder if she's made other friends and forgotten about me. And she promised ..."

"Have you written to her?" asked Papa.

"Once."

"I think you could write her again. You just have to keep knocking, and if they don't answer, you knock again. That's how I deal with stingy dukes and electors who are reluctant to part with their money. I refuse to give up."

Nannerl resolved to write Katherl when they reached Coblenz. She had a lot to tell her — about Sopherl and the Mannheim Orchestra, about the new clavier, about her symphony.

"Coblenz ahead!" shouted the captain. Nannerl squinted into the rain and saw the lights of the port. She stared at the high mansions that lined the riverbanks. "Do you know people here, Papa?"

"There is the Baron Kerpen," said Papa. "He is the French ambassador and I remember his family; seven sons and two daughters! And they all play one or two instruments!"

"When can we visit them?" asked Nannerl, thinking about the two daughters. "Are the girls my age?"

"No, they are all older than you and Wolfi," said Papa. "Most of them don't live at home any more. But they often come to visit their father. I will never forget the beautiful singing voice of one of the daughters — I think her name is Charlotte."

Charlotte — Nannerl felt as if she wanted to say the name aloud a few times. It was delicious, like chocolates or music.

The rain had stopped and Nannerl felt the nudge of the boat against the pier. She leaned over the railing and noticed some men in a boat fishing, others casting from the shore. She liked this port — the smells of fish and old wood, the people unloading boats or walking along the shore. There was a bustle of passengers in a hurry, and Papa went below in search of Mama and Wolfi and Sebastian and the trunks. Nannerl held onto the rail a little longer and looked out at the mist, not wanting to leave the boat and the way it made her feel like an explorer discovering new territory.

"C'mon Nannerl, I'll race you to the mail coach!" croaked Wolfi, coming up behind her and tugging at her sleeve. His face was chalk white and he had little dark circles under his eyes. Salome Musch dangled from his hand.

"Papa says you have a cold. I don't think you should run around. It'll just get worse," said Nannerl, trying to sound like Mama.

"Never!" he said, coughing a few times. "Catch me if you can!" He took off down the long ramp and Nannerl ran after him, passing him at the toll booth and beating him to the carriage by a few steps.

She was about to tease Wolfi about being a slowpoke, but then she noticed that he was having trouble breathing and she decided to keep quiet. She looked for Mama and Papa in the fog. She thought she could see their shapes. It was Mama's voice that she heard first. "Wolfgang! Nannerl! Into the coach, both of you! Wolfgang, you'll catch a worse chill than you already have if you stay out in this damp evening."

Nannerl stepped up behind her brother into the crowded coach. She squished herself between an old woman and the window. Papa and Sebastian sat across from her, and Wolfi snuggled up against Mama in the seat nearest to the door. A young woman with a high wig and stylish swishy silk skirts came in and sat across from Wolfi and Mama. Nannerl couldn't help staring. She had flowers in her hat swept exactly in the latest fashion, as Katherl had described them. She looked at Wolfi and clucked her tongue. "And where are you from, my little man?" she asked Wolfi, as the coach began to roll forward.

"I am from Salzburg," croaked Wolfi importantly, sitting up straight and pulling his shoulders back.

The woman laughed. "All the way from Salzburg — home of the famous Mozart children!"

Wolfi looked insulted. "But I am a Mozart. I am Wolfgang Amadeus Mozart of Salzburg!"

"Really! And where is your Papa?" asked the woman, quickly looking around the crowded mail coach. Her eyes landed on Papa. "Herr Mozart!" she exclaimed. "Do you not remember me? I am Charlotte — "

"Fraulein Charlotte Kerpen!" said Papa. "I didn't recognize you at first. The last time I visited, you were still a girl. How is your dear Papa?"

Charlotte laughed. "Busy, as usual. It seems that being the French ambassador means you are not allowed to sleep much. But he'll relax a bit for the next two weeks — we will all be home — all nine of us! There will be lots of music and food!" She had green eyes that reminded Nannerl of a lively minuet. "When can you come for a visit?"

Papa looked at Wolfi. "I'm afraid our young Wolfgang is rather sick — "

"Not really — " interrupted Wolfi, wiggling in his seat.

"We will be sure to visit, as soon as our Wolfi is well," announced Papa. "In the meantime, give my best regards to your Papa and brothers and sister."

"Of course," said Charlotte. She looked at Nannerl. "You must be Maria Anna. I look forward to hearing you play."

Nannerl wanted to say something funny to make her laugh, but she felt tongue-tied and shy and could barely manage to say thank you.

Papa cleared his throat. "Here is our inn — come, children, gather your things." He made a little bow to Charlotte. "It has been most pleasant, and I look forward to seeing you in a few days."

"Good evening, family Mozart!" said Charlotte with another laugh. She seemed to laugh after everything she said, and it made Nannerl want to laugh. While Papa and Sebastian organized the trunks, Nannerl looked up and saw Charlotte wave from the window as the coach pulled away.

The Mozarts stayed in their room over the next days. Outside it stormed; inside, Wolfi coughed from under his thick quilt. Nannerl sat by the fire and started a long letter to Katherl.

September 18, 1763

Dear Katherl,

I have so many things to tell you, I don't know where to start. I miss you! The first thing is that

Wolfi is sick and I'm terribly worried. Each cough seems longer and louder, and each time I hear it I think of all the times I've ... I don't know ... well, all the times I wished I didn't have him for a little brother. There, I've said it. But I know now that if anything happened to him ... well, I can't imagine what it would be like without him, that's all.

He still doesn't know I'm writing a symphony! I wonder if you have any ideas for it? I wrote a flute part that I wish you could hear. Maybe you can imagine one and when we see each other again we'll match them together. Katherl, you were right about it being too big! How silly I was back in Salzburg, to think it needed two choirs and hundreds of violins! I am making it much smaller. And I'm changing it all the time. I still hope that Johann Christian Bach will —

"Nannerl, Mama ... " Wolfi called weakly and started a long coughing fit. Nannerl turned from her letter and rushed over to his bed.

"Can I have some cold water?" he asked, pulling the quilt around him and curling up into a little ball. "I'm so hot."

Mama brought Wolfi some water and smoothed the damp curls away from his forehead. Papa stood over them and frowned. "Now his cough has turned to fever. We'll have to spare the money and send for a doctor. Plus there's lost money because he isn't well enough to perform. I'll take the servant and fetch a carriage." He turned and stomped out of the room.

Nannerl turned to Mama and swallowed hard. She had to ask. "Will he ... will he get better?"

"Of course," Mama said quickly, but her mouth was still tight. "Don't be silly. He just needs time to get over this temperature." She put a damp cloth on his forehead and stifled a yawn. She'd sat up with Wolfi the night before.

"Why don't you lie down and I'll look after him?" asked Nannerl.

"Nonsense, I can — "

"Please, Mama? I'd like to."

Mama stifled another yawn and shrugged. "I guess there's no harm. But wake me if he gets worse." She lay down and soon Nannerl could hear her steady breathing.

There wasn't much to do, really, except watch Wolfi toss and twist the blankets around himself. She forced herself to keep busy; otherwise she'd just worry. She put water on to boil and made him some coffee. She got a new cloth and soaked it in cold water.

"Nannerl?" Wolfi whispered as she placed it on his forehead.

"What is it? Do you want some more coffee?"

"Nannerl, I feel so achy, and these horrible chills are laughing and dancing all over me. I need music ... "

He started to groan. Nannerl's hand stiffened in mid-air. She just wanted to wake Mama, let Mama rub her back and say everything would be fine and Wolfi was better and the night and the rain and the fear lodged in her stomach would all go away. She got up to wake her.

"Music, Nannerl ... " Wolfi groaned.

Nannerl sat down again. Music. That's what she could do. She got Wolfi to lie on his stomach and rubbed his back in a rhythm, the way Mama rubbed hers. Then she started to hum, making up a tune to fit the slow rhythm. There was something of Salzburg in it — winter, a falling of snowflakes, grey cobblestones, the clop of a horse. She hummed in bits of Wolfi's laughter, the feel of his hand in hers, the way she could hear his heart when they played duets, even the awful ache she felt in her throat when everyone clapped for him. It seemed that she had been humming for hours when Papa and the doctor finally burst into the room.

"He was running a high fever — "

"Sh, Papa!" she whispered. "It took a long time to get him to fall asleep!" Nannerl couldn't believe the words that seemed to slip from her before she could stop them.

"Nannerl! Watch your tongue! I'm sure the doctor — "

"She's right," said the doctor, his hand on Wolfi's forehead. "He's finally sleeping, and his fever has dropped." He opened up his bag and handed Papa a bottle of dark red medicine. "Give him some of this if there's another fever. And this for the cough." He handed Papa another bottle. "But lots of rest is what he needs the most. How long have you been away from home?"

"Almost four months," answered Papa.

"Four months is a long time for young children to be on the road. Perhaps they need a vacation." He paused for a moment, as if he meant to say more. "Well, goodnight." He tipped his hat and left the room.

"I couldn't find anyone in Coblenz, had to search through the outskirts," said Papa, but Nannerl could hardly hear him. She was falling asleep thinking of Wolfi's fever tune, the one she would use in the slow second movement of her symphony.

❧ 10 ❧

THE KERPEN FAMILY ORCHESTRA

IT TOOK A WEEK BEFORE they could finally bundle Wolfi up in blankets and travel to the Kerpen residence for a visit. The estate lay outside Coblenz, high on the banks of the Rhine, so Papa hired a private carriage. Nannerl felt her stomach grow tight with excitement as they pulled into the steep driveway. She heard music as soon as she stepped into the hall.

"Good evening, Mozarts," boomed Baron Kerpen as he shook Papa's hand. "We are honoured to receive such esteemed guests. Please come to the music room to meet my children. That is, if they'll stop playing long enough to say hello. They've hardly stopped since they arrived."

Wolfi grabbed his violin and raced ahead.

"Wolfgang, your health — " Mama tried to hold him back, but she was too late. He was off in search of the music. Nannerl followed close on his heels, trying not to slip on the shiny floor. They stopped short at the open door to the music room, where candlelight flickered on the faces of the family orchestra. The sound of the violins and cellos and clavier stirred warmth into the autumn night. Then Charlotte stood and her voice poured through the room like golden syrup. The song ended in a whisper. There was a pause, and then they began to play a loud and lively dance.

Nannerl noticed Wolfi's head moving in time to the music. Suddenly he grabbed his violin, walked right into the centre of the circle and began to improvise. His small fingers flew over the fingerboard of his violin; his head and body danced. The ending was fast and furious and wild, like the wind through the high trees outside.

"Hooray!" shouted the Kerpen family when it was over, clapping and crowding around Wolfi.

"Herr Mozart, can we keep your son?" laughed Charlotte, taking Wolfi's hand. "We could make him a regular member!"

Nannerl hung back in the shadows with Mama. She wanted to jump up and laugh in the centre of the group, but instead she bowed her head, looked at the pattern on the floor and listened. She wished she could be like Charlotte, who didn't seem to care one bit about stuffy rules — being quiet and ladylike in the presence of strangers.

"Allow me to introduce everyone," said the Baron.

"Franz, my eldest son, and Wilhelm and Hugo. Anselm, Louis, Clara, Karl and Philipp. And of course you've already met Charlotte."

"Here, Maria Anna, Frau Mozart, come sit in front of the fire," said Charlotte, pulling up some chairs, while the others put away their instruments. Nannerl followed Mama across the room and sat down. She folded her hands in her lap, wishing that she was alone or with a friend like Katherl. A servant came around with steaming cups of cocoa and biscuits while the others took seats on chairs and on the floor before the fire.

"How wonderful to have such a fine orchestra, all in one family," said Papa. "Do you ever play in public, for money?"

"No, we prefer just to play at home," answered Charlotte. "Music is our way of speaking to each other and having fun. And how has your tour been? Did you get a chance to play for Maximilian the Third, the Elector of Bavaria?"

"Yes, the Elector paid quite a handsome sum for the two concerts that Wolfi and Nannerl gave," said Papa. "But we had to wait over a week to collect our earnings."

Charlotte frowned and scratched her head. She turned to the Baron. "Papa, wasn't it the Elector's sister, Frau Maria somebody, that lived near us, years ago, when we still lived in Paris?"

Nannerl's heart hammered in her ears, and she curled her fingers tight around her cup. The Elector's sister! Charlotte must mean Sopherl!

The Baron slowly nodded and looked into the fire. "You have a good memory, Charlotte. How many years has it been since we lived in that old house on the rue François?"

Charlotte sighed. "Paris ... if only Papa hadn't been transferred and we could live there still! It's such an exciting city. I can hardly wait to visit Grandmama and Uncle there this Christmas. Now I remember the name of the Elector's sister. Her name was Maria Sophia ... Maria Sophia Wenzel. Remember, her husband was that stern, handsome military officer?"

"But tell us, Papa," said one of the boys, "Wasn't there a story about her?"

The Baron kept his eyes fixed on the fire. When he finally spoke, it was in a slow, almost heavy voice. "What I know I heard from others, so I don't know if the story is completely true," he said. "But they say that Maria Sophia, or Sopherl as they called her, was a great musician in her day. Her brother, the Elector, composed and played the cello and she played the clavier and sang. They say that she held the crowds at Nymphenburg spellbound with her performances and that she was vivacious and charming — "

"Sort of like our Charlotte," one of the Kerpens said.

Charlotte leaned forward in her seat and fixed her green eyes on her father. "Do go on, Papa. I can't believe you're talking about the same person we lived next to for so many years!"

Nannerl pressed her fingers together. She wanted to tell Charlotte she had already met Sopherl at the Elector's dinner.

"Yes, well, as I was saying," continued the Baron, "she was the darling of Munich. Then one day, Lieutenant Wenzel came calling and she married him and they moved to Paris. And soon after, she stayed inside and never came out and hardly ever spoke to anyone — "

"Do you think he didn't let her?" asked Charlotte. "How perfectly awful. Caged inside like an animal — "

Nannerl thought of all the sound inside a clavier never being let out, or Wolfi's violin shut up in its case. She shivered, although the fire was warm on her legs.

"... and then she had a baby and it died, and then she had another, and it died as well."

"How absolutely tragic," said Charlotte, putting her hands on her hips and frowning at the Baron. "What happened to her awful husband?" Nannerl gasped a little. She thought he was awful, too, but to call a Lieutenant that in front of Papa and the Baron?

"He died a few years ago," answered the Baron. "So

now Sopherl grows old alone in the house on the rue François, still not speaking and rarely coming out."

Silence settled over the room. So that explained Sopherl's sad eyes, but what about her music? Had she kept playing inside the house? Nannerl thought that her head would burst with questions. She cleared her throat to speak.

"But ... but where is the rue François?" Nannerl's voice came out in a tiny squeak. "Is it in the centre of Paris?"

"Actually, it's on the outskirts, near the road that leads to the Palace of Versailles," said Charlotte. She gave Nannerl a puzzled smile. "Are you interested in streets and maps?"

Nannerl nodded, and Charlotte jumped up and grabbed her arm. "Come on," she said. "There's a map of Paris in Papa's study. I'll show you our old street."

Nannerl followed Charlotte up some stairs to a huge room filled with books and a very large desk. Charlotte opened a few drawers and shuffled through some papers.

"Charlotte ..."

"Yes?" Charlotte swirled around, a wrinkled map in her hand.

"I met Sopherl at the Elector's dinner."

"Really?" Charlotte sank into a chair.

"I asked her what instrument she had played and she

didn't answer," said Nannerl. "She heard me play and the Elector gave me her address and I want to see her in Paris and I suppose I'll have to ask Papa for help, but I know I need to visit her!"

"What an adventure! I wish I could come along! It would be fun to find Sopherl by yourself, don't you think? You're so clever — you don't need your Papa to help. Here, I'll show you. You see, there is the Seine, the river that flows through Paris." She traced her index finger along the edge of the river. "Here, at the great church Nôtre Dame, you turn left, past the Abbey of St Germain des Prés, along the rue de Sèvres for about fifteen blocks. Then you will come to the rue François, and our old house. It's really quite simple. I'm sure you'll be able to find it." She handed Nannerl the map. "We go to Paris every Christmas and know it well, from when we lived there."

"Thank you very very much," said Nannerl, taking the map and trying to hide her excitement. "There's one more thing ..." She had noticed a flute sitting up on one of the shelves.

"Yes?" Charlotte asked.

"Do you play the flute?"

Charlotte laughed. "Not officially." She took the instrument down. "This is Papa's. He plays along with our orchestra when he has the time. He's actually quite good. But — " she smiled at Nannerl and put the flute to her lips, " — he's given me a few lessons over the years. We're all so crazy about music in this house." She played a little tune.

Nannerl clapped. "If I sing something, could you play it back, just so that I can hear how it sounds on the flute?"

Charlotte laughed. "Of course! I'll do my best, anyway."

Nannerl closed her eyes and hummed the flute tune from her symphony. She was glad that she had changed it to fit with a smaller orchestra.

Charlotte played part of it back. "It's a very interesting tune. I like it. But I wonder about — " she played the last note a little longer, " — putting a pause there. Just to slow things down a bit, so the audience can really savour that note."

Nannerl thought about it. "Maybe," she said. "Can you play it that way again?"

"Nannerl!" Mama called from downstairs. "Come down now. It's time to go."

"Oh, bother," said Nannerl. She wanted to stay and work on her symphony with Charlotte.

"Never mind," said Charlotte. "I'm sure we'll meet again, perhaps in Paris at Christmas! Who is the composer of this wonderful melody?"

Nannerl just smiled and didn't say anything, but she knew that Charlotte knew who had written it.

"Keep working, Nannerl!" Charlotte whispered as they ran downstairs. "And good luck in finding Sopherl!"

"... yes, well, I'm sure we'll manage to get a concert at Versailles," Papa was saying as he buttoned his coat.

"Then we'll look forward to hearing Wolfgang and Nannerl play," said Charlotte, smiling. "We always go to the concert at Versailles on Christmas Day. It's a family tradition."

"Well, we really must get these children off to bed," said Mama hustling Wolfi and Nannerl out the door.

"Goodbye!" Everyone smiled and waved. "Come again before you leave Coblenz!"

Nannerl settled into her carriage seat for the long ride back to the inn. She peered out at the darkness and shivered. Then she reached deep into the pocket of her cape and felt the reassuring touch of her diary and Charlotte's map.

❦ *II* ❧

*W*AITING

*I*N PARIS, NANNERL PRACTISED scales. Her fingers ran up and down the keys, over and over, in time to the rain that pounded on the roof and mixed with the steady click of Mama's knitting needles. Nannerl had been practising all afternoon and now her legs felt cramped. She wanted to stretch them and take a long walk through a park. She wanted to find Sopherl. She got up suddenly, went to the window and sighed as she looked down at the people with their black umbrellas hurrying down the slick, grey street. It hadn't stopped raining since they had arrived two weeks ago and she was tired of staying indoors all the time!

She turned impatiently from the window and went over to Wolfi. He was seated at the table, writing in her diary. Usually Nannerl watched him while he wrote, but today she had wanted to practise, so Wolfi had solemnly promised not to look at her pages. Now she peered over his shoulder to see what he had written — in French, because that was the language she and Wolfi had used to write in the diary, ever since they had crossed the border from the Austrian Netherlands into France.

... and then a hoop from one of the wheels snapped. We had to wait at an inn for hours while the slow-pokes repaired it. We sat by the fireplace, where a kettle hung from a long chain and meat, turnips and other strange things all boiled together. We had a ragged tablecloth and ate soup and fish. All around us the people babbled a very bad French dialect. The funniest thing was the pigs — the door to the inn was constantly open and so the pigs wandered in and out as if they were guests! Snort, snort! And the largest looked exactly like the Count van Eyck!

"Wolfi!" Nannerl stifled a giggle. "You musn't say such things about the Count van Eyck, especially since he and the Countess are letting us stay here in their palace, and the Countess let us borrow her clavier with two key-boards!"

"But the Count does look exactly like those pigs, don't you think?"

Nannerl giggled. "Not nearly so much as that prince in Brussels. Remember, we had to wait almost a month to play for him, because he didn't have time. Remember how he was always hunting and eating and drinking?"

Wolfi sighed. "And now it looks like we'll have to wait just as long to get an invitation to play in Paris! I'm tired of waiting! I want to play a concert again!" He grabbed her diary and ran around the room.

"Wolfi!" cried Nannerl. "Give me back my diary!" She began to chase him. Wolfi stopped at a trunk and pulled out the miniature sword he had received from the Belgian prince. "You'll have to fight me for it first!" he cried, laughing and waving the sword.

"Children!" shouted Mama, putting down her knitting. "Stop that running this instant! And Wolfgang, you know better than to play with that precious sword! Put it back in the trunk where it belongs. I know it is hard, all this waiting, but — "

Papa suddenly burst into the room. Rain dripped from his wig and his cheeks were flushed.

"Three cheers for Herr Grimm!" he announced, triumphantly waving a small book in the air. "Now I am certain that the invitations for concerts will come rolling in, and so will the money! Just look at what Herr Grimm, the famous editor, has written about my children! And all of the intellectuals of Europe will read this literary journal!"

Wolfi dropped his sword. Nannerl took her diary from his hand and they both ran over to where Papa was standing. Nannerl looked over Papa's shoulder as he read.

True miracles are so rare that it behooves us to report one when it comes our way. A Kapellmeister of Salzburg named Mozart has just arrived here with two children who present the prettiest appearance in the world. His daughter, eleven years of age —

"But Papa, I'm twelve!" interrupted Nannerl indignantly.

"Yes, yes, Nannerl, but I told him to put both of your ages back a year. It's important that the public think you are as young as possible," answered Papa.

"But that's — "

"Nannerl, would you please let me finish?" said Papa. He cleared his throat and continued.

His daughter, eleven years of age, plays the clavier in the most brilliant manner, executing the longest and most difficult pieces with amazing precision. Her brother, who will be seven years old next February, is —

"I'm almost eight — "

"That's enough Wolfgang. Wait until you hear what he wrote about you!" He cleared his throat.

— who will be seven years old next February, is so

extraordinary a phenomenon that we can scarcely credit what we see with our own eyes and hear with our own ears. Easily and with utmost accuracy, the child performs the most difficult pieces with hands that are scarcely large enough to span a sixth. It is a wondrous thing to see him improvising for a whole hour, giving himself entirely to the inspiration of his genius and generating a host of delightful musical ideas, which, moreover, he unfolds successively with admirable ...

Nannerl stopped listening and looked out the window at the rain. Now the rest of the article would be about Wolfi. Papa's voice droned on and on, praising Wolfi and telling in great detail all the wonderful things he had done. Nannerl wanted to clamp her ears shut and run away. She felt something in the room, a kind of weight in Papa's words, pulling her shoulders and her head down to the floor. If only Papa would finish with the article!

... Mozart's children have aroused the admiration and wonder of all who have seen them. The Emperor and Empress have lavished kindness upon them, and they have enjoyed a similar reception at the courts of Munich and Mannheim. It is a pity

that in this country music is so little understood! The
father intends to proceed from here to England, and
then to take his children back home by way of North
Germany.

Papa beamed and snapped the book shut with a flourish. "Well, well, I shall expect important calls any time now. In the meantime, we must do something about our unfashionable German attire. When we do play these concerts, we want to look like proper Parisians! It is time for a shopping trip! Everyone prepare to go out of doors! I'll arrange a carriage! We're going to buy some French clothes!"

Wolfi and Nannerl ran to get their capes. Nannerl felt the weight drop away. New clothes from Paris! Wait until she told Katherl!

Mama stayed where she was and frowned at Papa.

"Leopold, I don't approve of the children walking about these Paris streets. The women are so unnatural-looking. Their painted faces and make-up would make any honest German blush! Perhaps you could go out alone — "

"Mama!" wailed Nannerl and Wolfi. Nannerl felt that she would burst if she didn't get out of this room soon.

"Come, Maria Anna," said Papa, holding open Mama's cape. "A short stroll through the business sector of Paris can do no harm. Besides, it is high time we showed ourselves off to the public."

Mama reluctantly got up from her chair and put on her cape. Wolfi and Nannerl raced down the stairs to the sitting room of the palace to wait. The Countess let them take one of her private carriages — once they were rolling along, Nannerl rubbed her hand against the foggy window and peered out at the distant spire of the famous Nôtre Dame cathedral.

In her head she went over Sopherl's address for what seemed like the hundredth time that week: *No. 68, rue François, Paris, France.* Every night since they had arrived, Nannerl had secretly taken out the map and traced the route from the van Eyck Palace to the rue François. Every night she resolved to find Sopherl the next day. But the next day always came and it seemed impossible to steal away from Mama and Papa and Wolfi. Nannerl shivered as she looked out at the winding maze of grey streets. Suppose she got lost? Suppose thieves and beggars lurked in the corners of the dark streets, waiting to kidnap her? But she must go ... soon ... she needed to find Sopherl.

The carriage rolled to a stop in front of the Champs Élysées, the famous street that was lined with trees and fancy shops.

"What good fortune," said Papa, stepping from the carriage first. "The rain has stopped for us." Mama quickly stepped down, linked her arm in Papa's and looked nervously at the crowds of people. She fidgeted with her gloves and looked down as she walked. Was Mama scared? In Germany, it had always seemed that Mama was the boss, at least in things like food and clothes and chores. But Mama hadn't had French lessons with Papa, the way Wolfi and she had. She looked lost and ... and well, plain ... in the crowds of people who rustled by in satins and silks, holding elegant fans even though it was almost December.

Nannerl couldn't stop staring at all the clothes; one woman had six huge feather plumes in her hat, all tied with a red satin bow that tilted stylishly above her left eye. Nannerl walked along, noticing that the skirts weren't as wide or as full as in Salzburg or the Netherlands; it must be the Paris style. She would have to remember to tell Katherl.

"Here we are," said Papa, ushering them into a shop filled with all kinds of fabric — red velvet and gold brocade, linen, satin, lace and silk. A man came towards them, but before he could say anything, Nannerl spotted the fabric she wanted for her dress. It was dark blue satin, the colour of evening, with thin gold stripes.

"I can see which fabric has caught this young girl's fancy," laughed the tailor, gently pulling a bolt of it off of the shelf and handing it to Nannerl. "It is in the very latest fashion. I can picture it as an overskirt, with this," he pulled down some white silk with tiny flowers dotted all over it, "as an underskirt. Perfect. Then white ruffles at the elbow, long gloves, a satin shoulder sash, a new taffeta hat, and she'll be set for Paris." He winked at Mama and Papa. Nannerl just stood there, cradling the blue fabric as if it were a child.

They went over to the full-length mirror and Mama and the tailor helped Nannerl to drape the material in front of herself. The colour and the satin made her look different — older, somehow.

"I must say," said the tailor, "she looks most exquisite in that particular shade of blue."

Papa came up from behind. "Nannerl will look far too old in that colour, and in the style you described," he said to the tailor. "We want her to look as young as possible, like an eleven-year-old."

"But Papa — " Nannerl began to argue.

"I insist on some other, simpler fabric — and a brighter colour! Why, you'll look like a young woman in those golden stripes! You must look the part of a child prodigy."

Wolfi came bounding over in a fancy black French hat. "*Bonsoir, Mesdames,*" he said, making a sweeping bow.

They all laughed and Papa inspected his watch. "Now, we must all have our measurements taken and select the appropriate fabric." He turned to the tailor. "How long will it take for the clothes to be ready?"

The man frowned and scratched his head. "About nine days at least, since I won't be able to start until the day after tomorrow."

"Very well," said Papa. "In nine days we'll be the most fashionable family in Paris!"

Nannerl stood like a statue and let the tailor measure the width of her shoulders and waist. He chatted about the fabric and the style Papa had chosen for her and she listened half-heartedly, glancing often at the deep blue satin lying like a forbidden jewel in the far corner of the room.

"... and you're sure he'll be stopping in Paris? Do you know how long he'll stay?" Papa was saying to an old man with bushy eyebrows at the front of the shop.

"Perhaps three weeks, perhaps four months ... one never knows with Johann Christian Bach."

"I had expected to meet him in London, where he lives, not so soon, not in Paris. Well, well, we will definitely prepare for his arrival. When did you say he would come?"

Nannerl let the tailor finish with the measurements, then rushed over to where Papa and the old man stood.

Papa put a hand on Wolfi's and Nannerl's shoulders. "Children, this fine gentleman from Munich has just told us some wonderful news; Johann Christian Bach will arrive in Paris in — "

" — a few days," finished the man. "I heard that he would most certainly be here in a few days."

That night, Nannerl worked on the final movement of the symphony in her tiny room at the palace. She wanted to finish it tonight — then she'd have a day or two to make final changes before showing it to Johann Christian Bach.

She looked at the candlelight flickering on the walls, still unable to believe that she had her very own room. Of course, it adjoined the main apartment and was barely big enough to hold a bed. But still, it was separate, with a real door and not just a partition separating her from Mama and Papa and Wolfi. On their arrival, the kind Countess van Eyck had looked Nannerl over and said, "I have just the room for you," and taken her up and shown her the room. No amount of protesting from Wolfi could change the fact that this room was hers.

Nannerl smiled to herself, hummed the violin part in the last movement and crossed out what she had written before. She had slowly been changing her symphony, ever since that evening with the Kerpen family. She wanted to make it simpler and more elegant. How silly she had been, to make it so huge, so clumsy, with all those instruments and choirs! This way, she might be able to hear her symphony performed.

But it took a long time to take instruments out and

polish the work until it gleamed like the silver in Mama's cabinet at home. She sighed and rested her pen in the inkwell. Just one stretch left. It was a violin duet finale — she wanted the two melodies to bump against each other at first, then sink together into a rhythm and slowly climb a very grassy hill, then fly ...

But how could she make the notes do that? She rocked back and forth in her chair and fiddled with her thumbs. She crossed her arms and uncrossed them. She sat very still for a few minutes with her eyes closed, listening to the melodies in her head. Then she dipped the pen and began to write, quickly, before the notes could slide away from her. Up, up a steep mountainside — she couldn't look down for dizziness but she knew she was near the top. Step after step, note after note until finally she felt the sun on her face and the whole symphony shimmering and finished below her. She rested her head on her arms, waiting for the last note to dry.

❦ *12* ❧

*A*n *U*nexpected *G*uest

Advent, Advent,
A little light burns.
First one, then two
Then three, then four
Then stands the Christ child
Before the door.

*N*ANNERL AND WOLFI SANG while Mama lit the four candles on the Advent wreath. They had sung the song of the Christ child during the candle-lighting ever since Nannerl could remember. On the last Sunday in November, Mama would light the first candle and then for three more Sundays in December she would light another candle, to mark the weeks left to Christmas. Nannerl closed her eyes and smelled the pine and the melted wax and pretended that she was five or six, back in Salzburg when Grandma Pertl was alive, in the days before they spent Christmases away.

She opened her eyes and saw that Mama was smiling.

"I have a surprise for your breakfast today," Mama said, hiding something behind her back.

"Marzipan!" shouted Wolfi.

"Not for breakfast, silly," said Nannerl. "*Baumkuchen*?"

Mama's eyes twinkled and she shook her head, then placed a loaf of *Christstollen* bread on the table.

"*Christstollen*! Much better than marzipan any day!" said Wolfi. Nannerl's mouth watered as she looked at the huge loaf smothered in melted butter and icing sugar. It really did look like the Christ child wrapped in swaddling clothes. As Mama began to cut it into sections, Nannerl saw that it was jammed with dried fruit and almonds. "Less than a week until Christmas Eve," said Wolfi, taking a big forkful of bread. "I hope St Nicholas brings us good things to eat!"

"I hope he brings us an invitation to play at the King's palace at Versailles," said Papa, frowning and sipping his coffee. In the past weeks, ever since the article had come out, Wolfi and Nannerl had given seven concerts in Paris. But they still waited for an invitation to play at the most important concert: the concert at the Palace of Versailles on Christmas Day. "Well, at least Johann Christian Bach is in the city and will visit us," Papa continued. "I expect him in three days, on December 22."

Nannerl's heart raced. Three days! Months ago, in Salzburg, when Papa had first mentioned Johann Christian Bach, Nannerl had been hoping that she as well as Wolfi would be able to see him. She had been wanting to show him her work for so long, and he would help her to get it published and played — after all, he was a real composer. Of course, Papa was only thinking of Wolfi. But maybe Herr Bach would be a kind man, and if she asked very nicely, he might look at her work as well as Wolfi's.

In the days that followed, Mama and the Countess van Eyck kept Nannerl busy in the kitchen. The Countess' French cook didn't know how to make German Christmas treats and the Countess was determined to celebrate the holiday the way she had when she was a girl in Salzburg. Nannerl loved the warm, spicy smell of the kitchen. On the day before the expected visit from Herr Bach, she sat slicing a roll of *Pfeffernüsse* dough into squares to make tiny, spicy cookies, thinking about the composer and wondering if he would really listen to her symphony. A loud knock sounded through the kitchen. Mama and the Countess had gone to the sitting room for afternoon coffee and Nannerl was alone. She wiped her hands on her skirt and jumped up to answer. No one important would knock at the back kitchen door. She opened it to a huge man with big grey eyebrows furrowed into what seemed a permanent frown.

"I'm looking for Wolfgang Amadeus Mozart, the young prodigy of Salzburg, and his father Herr Leopold Mozart. Are they at home?" he demanded in a gruff voice.

Nannerl tried to speak but her throat was so tight that she just stared. She was sure this was Johann Christian Bach. She had seen his portrait in the hall of the Salzburg court.

"Well, speak up," he said, taking out his watch. "I haven't got all day to stand here and stare at little girls with flour all over their skirts! Are the father and son at home or not?"

Nannerl found her voice, partly because she was angry that the man had been so rude.

"My father, Herr Mozart, was not expecting you until tomorrow," she said in her most dignified voice. "Please follow me and I will show you to the upper chambers."

Papa and Wolfi were sitting at the clavier. They turned at the sound of footsteps, and as soon as Papa saw the composer his cheeks grew red and he jumped up with his hand extended.

"Greetings, Herr Bach," he said. "I am afraid I was expecting you tomorrow."

"Never mind," the composer said briskly. He nodded at Wolfi. "This must be the prodigy. Very well, then, I should like to see him alone, if possible. My time is quite limited."

"Certainly," said Papa, bowing and motioning for Nannerl to follow him.

"Papa," whispered Nannerl. "May I please go to my room?"

Papa nodded and Nannerl ran to the door at the far end of her room. Once she was safely inside, she lay down on her stomach and propped her chin in her hands. Now what would she do? She hadn't expected Papa to include her, but she *had* bargained on the composer being nice enough to look at her symphony. She had it all planned; as soon as he was finished working with Wolfi, she would quietly present him with her pages of music and ask politely if he could tell her what she could improve. Simple. But not now, not this rude man with the hard eyes.

She looked at the pages of her symphony, sitting in a neat pile on the night table. The melodies were like good old friends to her now, like Katherl. She turned onto her back and hummed them softly, remembering the times when she had skipped walks or sightseeing excursions to bend over the clavier and compose. She remembered the clear sound Charlotte had made playing the melody from the third movement on the flute. She imagined the sound of the violin duet she had written in the finale and the way she had fought sleep in the last few days to finish it.

Something started to rise inside her. It started as a

tiny stream, way in the bottom of her big toe and slowly rose up through her legs and her chest until it seemed as huge as an ocean in her veins. It was something like anger, but no ... it was more like ... like the way she had felt that time when she had stood up before Papa to play the Eckhardt sonata at Schwetzingen Palace. Something had been bursting inside to get out and she just needed to step forward and let it out before anyone could stop her, before she lost her nerve.

Her symphony deserved to be heard. She would ask Johann Christian Bach to hear it. After all, that had been her original plan way back in Salzburg when she had first started to work on it. She got up from the bed and began to pace the small space. The sound of the clavier drifted in; fast sixteenth notes in the left hand and a soaring melody above them; Wolfi was improvising. She sat on the bed and then got up and looked out the window at the frozen garden and then paced some more. It seemed that she had been in the small room for hours and she wanted to get out.

She was just about to try writing in her diary when she heard a laugh. It was more of a low, gruff rumble than a laugh. Nannerl opened the door a crack and peeked out. Johann Christian Bach was smiling and Wolfi was sitting on his lap! They were playing a duet.

"My father, Johann Sebastian, used to take me on his

knee and we would play duets exactly like this," said Herr Bach as they played. They finished the grand finale and Wolfi hopped off the composer's lap.

"I am grateful to have heard you today, Herr Mozart," Herr Bach said in a reverent tone as he solemnly shook Wolfi's hand. "I expect to see much more of you. I would like to discuss your future with your Papa. Could you please run and get him?"

Wolfi ran off and the old man nodded and began to gather his things. Now was her chance. Nannerl took a deep breath and walked towards the clavier.

"Excuse me, Herr Bach," she began in a small voice, holding out her symphony in front of her. "I'm Nannerl, Wolfi's sister. I wondered if you ... well, if you possibly had some time, I've written a symphony ..."

There was a moment of silence. Then he began to laugh. It started with a rumble and grew bigger until his big guffaws filled the room. Nannerl's face grew hot and she bent her head to the floor.

"A symphony? So the little kitchen maid is composing a symphony? Well, well, I promise not to tell your Papa if you give me a few of those delicious cookies I smelled when I first arrived. A symphony! Ha, ha, ha." He glanced at his watch and quickly finished buttoning his coat. "Perhaps, someday, I will hear you perform one of my sonatas. I hear you are quite a precise little player.

But today I really must run. There's a grand concert at the hotel tonight and I am the guest of honour. Good day, my dear." He gave her a little bow and swept out of the room.

Nannerl stood rooted to the floor. She felt like the statue in the Salzburg town square. She hoped that she would never have to move again. She didn't want to eat *Christstollen* or hug Wolfi or lick icing sugar off her fingers or see a sunset ever again. She didn't want to hear music any more either, or play it, or roll in the grass and smell roses. A page of her symphony slowly fluttered from her hand to the floor. Another followed and then another, until the entire work lay in a messy heap at her feet. She heard footsteps on the stairs; light footsteps, taking two steps at a time. Wolfi's footsteps. He came running into the room.

"Hey, Nannerl, where were you? Johann Christian Bach and I played some really great — "

"Stop it!" Nannerl shouted, covering her ears. "Just stop it! I hate you and I never want to see you again in my whole life!" She burst into tears, gathered up the pages in her arms, ran into her room and slammed the door.

She sobbed until her head ached. Then suddenly, like the birds at five o'clock in the morning announcing the dawn, she knew that she had to see Sopherl. It had been over a month since they had arrived in Paris. She didn't just want to have an adventure, as Charlotte had said. Right now, more than anything else in the world, Nannerl wanted someone to listen to her symphony. Sopherl would help her. To think that she had actually hoped Johann Christian Bach would help to get it published!

"Nannerl, come and help with supper." Mama was calling from the kitchen. Nannerl's head pounded as she got up from the bed. She straightened her dress and ran down to help Mama.

During supper, she and Wolfi didn't look at each other or say a word but Papa didn't seem to notice anything different. He babbled on about the concert invitation to the Palace of Versailles that he had just received.

"We will leave for Versailles on December 24 and attend Christmas Eve Mass at the Royal Chapel. Then, on Christmas Day, my children will play for King Louis XV of France! At last, the invitation I have been waiting for. Wolfgang, Herr Bach was extremely impressed with you and recommended that I take you to Mass at the big cathedral tomorrow night. He thinks you should have exposure to the motet form and there is an excellent choir singing one there. I only wished I had thought of teaching you about the motet a long time ago."

Nannerl ate her potatoes and red cabbage and said nothing. Then she quietly helped Mama to clean up the dishes and was about to run to her room when Papa stopped her. He smiled.

"In all the excitement over Versailles, I forgot to give you this," he said, pulling out a thin envelope from behind his back.

"Katherl!" shouted Nannerl, forgetting for a moment about the horrible afternoon and Johann Christian Bach. "Thank you, Papa," she said as she grabbed the letter and raced up the stairs to her room.

She tore it open and unfolded a thin piece of paper.

December 1, 1763

Dear Nannerl,

I am so very very sorry for not writing sooner. Please forgive me? So many times I began a letter and then something would distract me or I wouldn't be in quite the right mood and I would throw it onto a pile with all the other halfway finished letters.

Thank you ever so much for your letters. Your adventures sound wonderful! You must tell me about all the fashions of Paris. I have been busy helping Mama, but also something else. A theatre group has been visiting Salzburg for the past two months and I often go to watch. How I would love to be a part of it! I know all of the players quite well now, and often do some acting with them, just for fun, at rehearsals.

You asked me to help you with the missing link of your symphony and I realize that although I made that vow in your room that day, I wouldn't know where to begin to help with the musical part. All I can say is that you have to share your music! If you're finished your symphony, you should perform it at your very next concert, and not bother about publishing and Johann Christian Bach and all that.

Who cares what they think? You just need to show what's inside yourself. You need to show Nannerl to them, my friend Nannerl who is honest and kind and interesting. Anyway, I must go now. The Hagenauer family is coming for afternoon coffee!

    Love,

    Katherl

PS Say hello to your Mama and Papa and pinch Wolfi on the cheek for me!

Nannerl slipped into her nightshirt and snuggled under the covers. Katherl was right. The most important thing now was to let this music inside of her out. Well, she had, in the symphony. But what good were a bunch of notes written on paper? Katherl had said to play it at her very next concert. Versailles. Charlotte had told her the whole Kerpen family would be there. Was it too much of a dream to think that they could play it? Their orchestra could play it, now that she'd changed it so much.

She thought of Papa's disapproval of her improvising and writing music and playing certain instruments. Johann Christian Bach's laugh echoed loud and long in her head. Then the sound of her symphony took over. Maybe she really could get the Kerpens to play it. People might hate it and laugh as Herr Bach had done. Well, she would have to take the chance. And tomorrow, when Papa took Wolfi to Mass, she would visit Sopherl!

𝒜 𝒱IOLIN ℒESSON

𝒩ANNERL CLUTCHED HER MAP and ran through the cold mist. She was pretty sure of where she was going. If only there weren't so much darkness on either side of her and such a long, empty space between each pale street lamp. She finally reached one lamp and stopped to check the map. She was heading down a side street off the rue du Temple towards Nôtre Dame. She paused for a moment and heard the muted cathedral bells through the swirling mist. Papa and Wolfi would be there now, listening to the motet.

An hour earlier, after Wolfi and Papa had climbed into the carriage and left for Mass, Nannerl had pretended to write in her diary. But she had really been too nervous to do anything but sit. Then Mama had got up from her knitting and announced that she didn't feel well and was going to retire early, and that Nannerl should also go to bed soon and not wait up for Wolfi and Papa. Nannerl couldn't believe her luck — after all this waiting, she was finally alone! When she was sure Mama was asleep, she had grabbed her cape, shoved her symphony into one of Papa's carrying cases and ran out of the palace through the back kitchen door before she had time to change her mind.

Now she was still running. Pounding hooves approached from behind and she turned and saw a carriage racing towards her. She ran faster. What if they stopped and asked her what she was doing? What if she were caught by strangers? But the carriage went by, leaving a fine spray of mud and the smell of horses and manure. She felt the mud on her face and coughed and ran on, slowing a bit because her lungs felt tight. Would she never get to Sopherl's house? It seemed that she had been running on this dark street forever.

Nannerl could see flickering lights ahead. She began to walk as she turned a corner and neared a building with many storeys. Carriages slowed to a stop in front of the huge front doors. Ladies and gentlemen in evening finery alighted with the assistance of footmen. Nannerl saw the name Hôtel above the door. She wanted to stop for a rest and peer through the windows at all the silk dresses and food and tinkling glass bathed in candlelight, but she rushed on. The doorman seemed to be staring straight at her!

Nannerl hurried away from the hotel and ran to a street lamp, where she could check the map again. Now she must cross a bridge — the pont Nôtre Dame. She looked up from the map and saw it arch like a great black cat in the mist that hovered over the Seine River. What if — no, she must stop scaring herself with questions about what might happen. She took a deep breath and walked over to where the stone bridge began. There was a wide walkway. Nannerl could hear the foaming, swirling mass of black water beneath her, washing up against the bank. She forced herself not to look down over the railing until she was safely over on the other side.

Now she was in the square of the Nôtre Dame cathedral. She looked up to see the spires reach into the mist like slender fingers. As she got closer, she could hear the thundering organ and the voices of the choir. What if the Mass finished and Wolfi and Papa got home before she could? But no, Papa had said it would last for hours. Still, she should hurry. She tried to run but her legs ached and she could only keep up a kind of walking trot.

Suddenly, Nannerl felt a sharp tug at the bottom of her cape. Her heart beat harder, throbbed fast through her arms and legs and face as she looked down. There, crouched up against the side of the church was a woman reaching a hand towards her. Nannerl wanted to run but she couldn't move.

The woman leaned forward in the darkness. "A sou, Mademoiselle, a few sous for some bread," her raspy voice rose. Though she couldn't have been older than Mama, the woman's eyes were ancient. Another bony hand reached for her dress, and Nannerl saw people crouched all along the cathedral wall; their cries for bread, a sou and shelter from the cold drifted through the mist. Nannerl caught the sharp stench of urine.

She found a coin in her pocket and placed it in the woman's hand. "Bless you, Mademoiselle," a voice said. Nannerl didn't answer. She ran as fast as she could, away from the smell and the quavery hands. Her legs felt like the stubs of candles but she didn't care. She ran on and on, past street lamp after street lamp.

She stopped to catch her breath. In her hurry to get away from the beggars she hadn't paid attention to the street signs. She tried to smooth out her map and see where she was. Her hands were still shaking with fright and cold and the lines on the map seemed to crisscross at the wrong places. Where was the rue de Sèvres, the one she needed in order to find the rue François? Had she turned the wrong way at Nôtre Dame?

Two dogs came sniffing around her heels. She wanted to run away from them, but knew she should stay and figure out where she was. They circled and sniffed. She told herself that they wouldn't bite; they were just ordinary dogs like Bimberl. She looked up and saw an old man with a cane hobbling towards her.

"Excuse me, I wonder if you could tell me where the rue de Sèvres is?" she asked in her best French. He just looked at her, frowned, motioned with his arms somewhere in the direction she had come and hobbled on, the dogs barking and following on his heels. She sat down on a nearby bench. As the mist drew in closer, she realized that she was lost in the middle of Paris. She wanted to just sit and rest and hope for help, but she forced herself up from the bench and back in the direction of the church.

She started to run, the tears on her cheeks mixing with the mud and the mist. Then, after blocks and blocks of darkness she spotted the Abbey of St Germain des Prés. Charlotte had said the rue de Sèvres was nearby! She saw the street sign — rue de Sèvres! She turned left and ran on, feeling new energy in her legs. She peered at each sign, hoping it would be the rue François. Maybe Charlotte had given the wrong directions. She had said fifteen blocks and Nannerl had already counted eighteen since turning onto the rue de Sèvres.

Then the sign for the rue François rose from the mist and Nannerl wanted to shout with triumph. She turned and ran down the street, searching for Sopherl's house. She spotted a tiny sign hidden behind a bush in front of a long, winding driveway — No. 68! Her stomach grew tight as she approached the mansion. It wasn't like the van Eyck Palace, where her family was staying, but it had a large garden with rows of trees lining the front walk. Nannerl breathed a sigh of relief when she saw the lights that burned inside. She must hurry ... in a few hours Mass would be over and she still had to walk back!

She grabbed the large front knocker and gave three loud raps. The door finally creaked open and a thin man with a sour face stood before her. He frowned as he looked her over. Nannerl realized how ragged she must look, with her face and cape all splotched with mud.

"May I help you?" he asked in a voice that was as thin as himself.

"I'm looking for So — , I mean Frau Wenzel," said Nannerl. The butler just stared at her.

"I ... I've met Frau Wenzel before, at her brother's palace at Nymphenburg," she said. "I need to see her." Now that she had stopped running, the moisture on Nannerl's skin turned cold and she began to shiver. The butler motioned for her to come inside.

"Wait here," he said and disappeared up a long flight of stairs. The front hall seemed starched and unused, like a museum. She peered around the corner to investigate the sitting room. A large clavier painted with intricate designs stood in the corner.

She looked up at the sound of light footsteps. Sopherl was coming down the stairs, slowly, one at a time, until she stood on the bottom stair and looked at Nannerl with the strange, sad eyes that Nannerl remembered from the dinner. She noticed the tiny wrinkles around Sopherl's eyes and mouth and saw how she always seemed to be twisting her hands. Somehow, she had expected Sopherl to make everything all right, to wave a wand and make her symphony published, to help her not be scared to say what she really thought to Papa and to make people notice her instead of Wolfi all the time. But now there was just this old woman standing before her, nervous and silent.

"My name is Maria Anna Walburga Ignatia Mozart, well, actually most people just call me Nannerl. We met at your brother's palace at Nymphenburg," Nannerl whispered, afraid she would break something if she spoke any louder. "I ... I'm sorry if I've come at such an odd hour and without an invitation ... I ... um ... well, I ran here alone. My Mama's at home asleep and my brother and Papa are at Mass ..." Her voice began to break and she felt that any moment she would start crying again.

Sopherl patted her on the shoulder and took her cape. "Of course I remember you. Nannerl — how could I ever forget your improvisations on that Bach sonata? I was hoping to meet you again. Follow me to the kitchen," the older woman said. Her voice was creaky with disuse, like an old door hinge. In the kitchen, a bright fire flickered and Sopherl motioned for Nannerl to sit by it. She told the cook to bring them tea, sat down by Nannerl and looked into the fire.

"After that dinner ... I ... I kept wondering about you. And your brother — he, he said we could help each other," Nannerl tried to explain again. "He said ... he told me never to stop playing. Never. That my music reminded him of you and that I should visit you." Nannerl's voice died, and then the only sound was the fire and the rattle of the cook preparing the tea and the distant tick of a grandfather clock. "I've written a symphony," she continued, determined to fill the silence. "A symphony. I did. It used to be huge with lots of instruments but now I've decided to make it the right size to be performed. I took out the choirs. Too many violins. I kept having to change different parts, to fit the new way I was thinking about it — "

Sopherl nodded. "Change," she said, and rocked a bit in her chair. "Not easy, I should think, to change one's ideas and then do something about them." She was silent for a while, then looked at Nannerl. "But if anyone can do it, it's you," she said, and her voice suddenly gained force. "Your long trill in that Bach sonata pulled me into rooms with brilliant colours and shapes I'd never seen. I knew then that you are one who is not afraid of change...." Her voice trailed off.

"You're right, about it not being easy," said Nannerl, settling in her chair. She was starting to like this kitchen, the distant ticking of the clock. "I heard a flautist in the Mannheim orchestra, and had an idea and worked and worked to change the flute part, and then Charlotte heard it and thought maybe something else should change, and my friend Katherl — well, she just thinks the whole thing should be played! I wanted Johann Christian Bach to see it but he had to hurry off to the hotel and only laughed. I have it here. Do you think I could possibly show it to you? That is, only if you want ..."

"I am not accustomed to music any more," said Sopherl, looking down at her lap. "But I suppose it wouldn't do any harm to listen...."

"You will then? You'll listen to it?" Nannerl opened Papa's carrying case and grabbed the pages of her symphony. She followed Sopherl to the sitting room, ran to the clavier and propped up the pages. She looked over at Sopherl, standing like a statue in the doorway. Then she played what she could, finding the main melodies and filling in the rest of the parts. She was at the end of the first movement when she saw out of the corner of her eye that Sopherl had come over to stand behind her.

Nannerl sang the violin melody of the slow second movement, wanting Sopherl to hear about Wolfi's fever, his steady groans in the darkness. She played the flute melody in the last movement, trying to remember the sound Charlotte had made. She frowned when she came to the finale, the violin duet, because it was almost impossible to play two lines on the clavier and capture the spirit of it.

Then a real violin played the part for her. She turned and saw Sopherl with a violin under her chin, her eyes fixed on the music, her fingers flying over the fingerboard like Wolfi's. Sopherl played the violin! The sound was a bit squeaky at first, like Sopherl's voice. But it grew rich and full as the symphony drew to a close.

When they were finished, Sopherl sat down on the bench next to Nannerl and sighed. "Thank you, Nannerl," she whispered in her soft, rusty voice. "People don't remember the way I used to play the violin. Some might remember the clavier and my voice, but it was the violin that I loved to play. My brother and I used to play duets late into those summer nights at Nymphenburg Palace. My father didn't mind. Of course, I never performed the violin in public, but the rest of the time, my violin was here." She pointed to a tiny faded scar just under her chin, where the violin must have rubbed against her skin.

"That was what you meant with your left hand, when you changed it from a fist to a violinist's hand!" Nannerl rounded the fingers of her left hand like a violinist and held it out towards Sopherl. "At the dinner, you were answering my question! You played the violin!" Sopherl smiled and nodded.

"But why did you stop?" asked Nannerl.

Sopherl twisted her hands for a long time before she answered, and Nannerl was scared she would turn silent again. "My husband, Herr Wenzel, didn't like it that I played so many instruments," she finally said. "He got especially angry when I played the violin. Maybe he eventually forbade me to play it because I preferred to spend more time with it than with him!" Her little laugh was like bitter coffee. "Why did I ever obey him? All those years." She shook her head. "But that day, after I closed my case for the last time, it seemed as if my own voice and laughter and everything that I loved to do was trapped inside the case with the violin.... I've thought about opening it again, since he died. But I don't think I had the courage ... it's been twenty-five years since I played." She took a sheet of Nannerl's symphony and studied it. "But you ... you and your beautiful music helped me to play and speak again." Sopherl's voice seemed to brighten like the tone of her violin.

"Would you like to learn how to play?" Sopherl got up from the bench with her violin. "This will be too large for you, but I'm afraid that my smaller violin is at Nymphenburg Palace, locked up in a closet somewhere."

Would she like to play! Nannerl let Sopherl place the instrument on her left shoulder. "There's a story I've been told so many times," she said as Sopherl helped to curl her fingers around the bow. "When Wolfi was just little, about four, Papa and his friends were sight-reading some trios and Wolfi begged to join. 'You don't need to take lessons to play second violin!' he'd said. He hadn't had any instruction on the violin and Papa said no, but one of the players let Wolfi play with him and soon tears were running down Papa's cheeks, he was so amazed at Wolfi."

"Now you'll be able to do the same thing!" said Sopherl. Nannerl nodded and practised moving the bow in the air. Of course, she'd sneaked Wolfi's violin and bow a few times to try. But most of the time she'd just watched — very closely, whenever Wolfi or Papa played. She'd memorized how to hold the bow, how to work the left fingers.

"Go ahead, draw the bow across the string quite quickly, so it won't make the sound crunch," instructed Sopherl. There were a few squawks at first, but after a few minutes Nannerl felt easy with the violin, as if she had always played. So this was what Wolfi had felt that time! It was as if she were going back inside that story, only this time Papa and his friends weren't here to listen and cry and marvel in amazement.

"That's fine!" said Sopherl. "Here, try the second violin

part from the duet in your symphony." It was a bit tricky trying to make her fingers fall exactly where she heard the pitch, but soon she got the hang of it. Nannerl looked over at Sopherl. She would perform this at Versailles before King Louis XV on Christmas Day! All she needed was somehow to get the Kerpens to help! But what would Papa and everybody else say? She tried not to think of that as she finished the duet part and put the violin down.

"That was fine, Nannerl," said Sopherl. "You just need to practise a little every day. But tell me, how did you ever find me? You said my brother gave you the address, but the directions ..."

"It was the Kerpen family, from Coblenz. Charlotte said that you used to be neighbours."

"The Kerpens! Do you know that they're here in Paris now?" asked Sopherl. "They're staying at a hotel because their poor old grandmother is too weak and tired to have the whole clan at her house."

Nannerl nodded. "The instruments they play just about match the ones in my symphony!" She squeezed her hands in excitement. "They can help me perform my symphony at Versailles on Christmas Day ... and maybe you can play the first violin part in the duet at the end!"

"A splendid idea!" said Sopherl. "Except the part about me playing." She lifted the violin, brushed some rosin dust off the fingerboard and then put it down again. "Franz Kerpen can play," she said. "He's very gifted and I'm too old to play for people. I'll play my violin at home now, thanks to you — but not for the King and all the musicians of Paris!"

Nannerl wanted Sopherl to play, but she saw from the taut line of Sopherl's mouth that it was useless to beg. "Do you really think I could ask the Kerpen family to play? I remember, Charlotte said it was a family tradition for them to attend the Christmas Day concert at Versailles. But how can I plan it?"

"I'll make sure they get the message to bring their instruments to Versailles and help you! I can deliver it myself to their hotel. It will be good for me to get out."

"Can you tell them what instruments I need?"

"Here — why don't you write them a message and then list the instruments." Sopherl handed her a quill pen and paper and Nannerl sat down and began to write.

Dear Kerpen Family,

My name is Maria Anna Walburga Ignatia Mozart and I met you in September at your home in Coblenz. I have written a symphony and would like to perform it at Versailles on Christmas Day. Could you please bring your instruments? It shouldn't be too difficult to sight-read. I would be very grateful if you could help me perform my work. With many thanks,

> *Yours truly,*
> *Maria Anna Walburga*
> *Ignatia Mozart (Nannerl)*

Nannerl listed the instruments. Maybe the Baron could play the flute, if he'd brought it with him to Paris. But who could play the organ? Well, she'd think about that later.

She handed the message to Sopherl. "They'll do it," Sopherl said. "This is a wonderful symphony. It deserves to be heard. I wish you much luck, my friend." She kissed Nannerl on the forehead.

Suddenly Nannerl remembered what time it was. What if Mass were finished and Papa had come home and found her bed empty! "Thank you so much for everything," she said. "But now I really must be going. You see, I left the house without anyone knowing — "

"Of course, poor child. Where did you come from?"

"The van Eyck Palace. You see, the Countess is a friend of Mama and Papa's, from Salzburg — "

"You'll catch a deathly chill before you play one note of your symphony if you walk back tonight. And it's almost eleven o'clock! Here, I'll get my coachman to hitch up the horses and take you home!"

Nannerl gathered the pages of her symphony and packed them in Papa's case. Then she sat in a chair to wait, her heart pounding hard. She couldn't stop planning the performance of her symphony.

Sopherl returned with a fur muff and some cookies. "Here. You must be starved. The driver is waiting in the front with the carriage."

"Thank you again," said Nannerl, waving goodbye to Sopherl as she walked into the chill mist. "Will you come to hear my symphony, even if you don't play?"

"We'll see," said Sopherl with a smile as she closed the door.

At home again, after she had thanked the driver, Nannerl sneaked back into the palace through the quiet kitchen. Lights still burned; the Countess must still be awake. Nannerl tiptoed quietly upstairs to her family's apartment and saw that Wolfi and Papa's cloaks were still missing from the rack. She got ready for bed, crept under the covers and lit a candle.

December 23, 1763

Dear Diary,

Sopherl helped me! I played the violin! It was the most delicious feeling — I can't describe it. And I can't stop thinking about playing my symphony at

*the Versailles concert! I suppose I'll have to ask Wolfi
if I can borrow his violin. I need to practise before
the concert. But he's still mad at me for the way I got
mad at him yesterday. I don't blame him. After all,
it wasn't his fault. I was just mad and jealous
because Herr Bach listened to him and not me. I
don't really hate Wolfi!*

*Maybe, if I ask nicely, he'll play the organ part
to my symphony! I'll just have to trust —*

Nannerl heard the sound of footsteps and quickly
snuffed out the candle. She let her diary fall to the floor,
turned to the wall and squeezed her eyes tight, pretending to sleep.

"Well, my boy, I expect you to compose a motet a
week — from now until we reach London," Papa was
saying as they put away their coats and got ready for bed.

"Those motets got a bit boring," said Wolfi. "But the
choir was good, even though the director stuck his nose
in the air too much."

Nannerl heard light footsteps approaching her room.
Then the door clicked open and she could feel someone
standing by her bed. Wolfi or Papa ... she heard the brush
of a coat against the quilt and then he was gone, closing
the door behind him. Maybe it had been Wolfi — he was
so strange sometimes. But she really wasn't mad at him

any more. She would apologize tomorrow and maybe he would agree to play the organ in her symphony. She fell asleep remembering how Sopherl's violin had felt under her chin.

❧ 14 ❧

ƲERSAILLES

"ℳAMA, CAN I PLEASE just have a taste of the marzipan you made?" Wolfi begged. He hopped down from the clavier stool and ran over to where Mama packed a trunk full of Christmas baking. "I'm starving, Mama, please?"

"Wolfgang," Mama scolded, "you know very well that on Christmas Eve we fast; now is the time to feel hunger. Tonight we will eat a bit of fish. But tomorrow ... tomorrow on Christmas Day at the grand banquet at Versailles, you may eat as much as you like!"

"I guess I can wait a little longer," said Wolfi. He ran back to the clavier and started practising again.

Nannerl's stomach rumbled as she listened to Wolfi's music and packed the trunk with candles and quilts. She hated the carp they had to eat every Christmas Eve. She could already taste its fishy bitterness on her tongue. On Christmas Day she would eat lots of marzipan, the sweets Mama made from almonds, to get rid of the taste of carp.

"Hurry with that packing, Nannerl," said Mama. "Papa and Sebastian will soon be back with the carriage and we still have to pack the clothing trunks."

Nannerl tucked a few candles into the trunk and sighed with impatience. This morning she had woken up and realized that she must copy out a separate part for every instrument that would perform her symphony! Right now she just had a full score; all the instruments together on one page. But everyone couldn't squish together and try to read off of the same score. They each had to have their own part, neatly copied, like the Mannheim orchestra. But when would she copy out all the parts? And who would play the organ? And how would she find a violin to play? She looked at Wolfi bent over the keys of the clavier, his tongue sticking out a bit as he concentrated on his sonata. She would have to make up with Wolfi.

Papa and Sebastian came into the room. "We really must hurry," said Papa with a worried frown. "I want to make sure that there is room for us at the Versailles hotel and we must have time to get settled and have our Christmas Eve supper before Mass." He went over to where Nannerl was tucking in the last corner of a quilt. "Is this trunk ready, Nannerl?" asked Papa.

"Yes, Papa," said Nannerl, letting the lid bang shut. She looked over at Wolfi, still practising as if he had never heard Papa enter the room. "Papa, if Wolfi packed his own clothing trunk instead of me packing both his and my own trunk as I usually do, don't you think things would go so much faster?"

Papa raised his eyebrows and scratched his head a bit. "But Wolfgang must have time to — " He stopped and looked at Nannerl for a while. Then he went over to the clavier and tapped Wolfi on the shoulder. Wolfi looked up at Papa and frowned.

"We must leave for Versailles soon, Wolfi," said Papa. "Please come and pack your clothing trunk so that we can get ready — "

"But Papa, Nannerl always packs mine and I have to practise," argued Wolfi. His lower lip began to stick out in a pout.

"There will be no arguing, Wolfgang," said Papa. "You will pack your trunk and that's that."

Wolfi sat at the clavier for a while with his arms folded. Then he stomped over to the wardrobe, grabbed his little coat and vest and shoved them in an empty trunk. Nannerl looked over at Mama and saw her smile a little. Then she gave Nannerl a quick wink and bent down to her packing.

In the carriage on the way to Versailles, Wolfi pressed his nose against the glass and stared out at the rain with his back to Nannerl. She hated this silence between them. She didn't want to make up just so that he would play in her symphony — she wanted to hug him and be friends again. But being the first one to give in was like forcing yourself to get out of bed at four in the morning and splash cold water on your face.

Maybe she didn't have to speak. She rapped out four quarter notes and two half notes on the bench, her and Wolfi's secret code for "I'm sorry and let's be friends." Wolfi kept his nose to the glass. She rapped it again, louder. This time he turned to her and tapped back — four sixteenth notes and a triplet, meaning "I have something to tell you later." Then he crossed his eyes and made his crabby Frau Spiegel face and Nannerl giggled. It hadn't been that hard after all. But it didn't feel right. Wolfi still seemed far away.

She peered over his shoulder and saw that the rain had stopped and the pale afternoon sun was beginning to shine through the clouds. Ahead were the dark outlines of buildings. Her hands started to go clammy. This must be Versailles!

"Papa, look!" she said, jumping up and almost bumping her head on the ceiling of the carriage. She pointed over Wolfi's shoulder and everyone gathered around the window to look out.

"Versailles, at last!" said Mama. They entered the village. Nannerl looked down the maze of streets curving off the main drive and glimpsed rows of large buildings and parks and more fountains.

Wolfi was squirming and twisting and hopping up and down in his seat. "Will we get to the palace soon, Papa; can we go inside it?" he asked.

"First we must get settled at the hotel, Wolfgang. Tomorrow you will see the palace, perhaps even the famous hall of mirrors, and tonight, after our Christmas Eve supper, we will have Mass at the royal chapel."

"You mean like the hall of mirrors that we saw at Nymphenburg?" asked Nannerl.

"Yes. Except this one is even wider and more elaborate. Everything at Versailles is grand," answered Papa. The carriage turned and pulled up before a building with three storeys. "Ah, here we are," said Papa. "May our stay here be successful and not too expensive."

Mama and Wolfi and Nannerl waited on a fancy couch in the lobby while Papa arranged things with the clerk. Everyone looked rich. Women came in through the wide doors wearing capes trimmed with fur and fur in their hair instead of flowers, and a lady came in wearing a little band of fur around her arm!

Papa walked towards them, frowning. "We'll end up spending more money at Versailles than anywhere in Europe! The clerk has just informed me that a single log of firewood costs five sous! And we must travel in sedan chairs here; every drive costs twelve sous and we must hire at least three of them." He sighed, then straightened up and adjusted his wig. "Come along, children, Maria Anna — there is much to do before Mass."

Nannerl followed Papa up the stairs to their room. Sedan chairs! She had never ridden in one, but she had seen them sometimes in Paris. You sat inside a fancy box with a window, with poles on either side. Two men, one in the front and one in the back, lifted the poles and carried you around. And Papa would be hiring three! Maybe she would get to travel in one alone, like a real rich lady!

It seemed to take hours to unpack, but at least Papa made Wolfi unpack his own trunk this time. The room was quite small and Nannerl had a little partition with her own bed like the one she had had in Munich. She quickly hung up her dresses in the wardrobe. In all of the excitement about Versailles she had forgotten about her symphony and the parts she had to copy. It would take hours and hours and when could she do it? She took the pages out from the bottom of the trunk and felt panic as she looked at all of the notes.

"Come, children. We must go down for supper," Mama interrupted her thoughts.

"Yes, Mama," said Nannerl, carefully hiding her music under the bed. She slowly followed Mama and Papa and Wolfi down the stairs and into the tavern, where Papa chose a table by the fire and ordered the horrible carp. Nannerl wrinkled her nose when she thought of eating it. She looked out the window and saw the distant rows of lights that must be the Palace of Versailles.

During supper, Nannerl remembered how in Salzburg on Christmas Eve she had always passed her carp down to Bimberl under the table. She felt an ache in her throat when she thought of Bimberl with the Hagenauer family. And it would be years before she could see her again!

"I miss Bimberl and Katherl and Salzburg," she announced.

"I miss Bimberl and Herr Hagenauer but not Frau Spiegel," added Wolfi.

"Never mind missing Salzburg, children," said Papa, getting up from the table. "You must remember the concert tomorrow, and playing for the King and Queen of France! Nannerl, what will you play?"

Nannerl's heart began pounding. How could she tell Papa that she would be playing her symphony? That is, if she could get the parts copied and if everybody showed up with their instruments. "Um — "

"I would like you to play the difficult Eckhardt sonata that you played at Schwetzingen," ordered Papa. "That composer Schobert who was so jealous of your Eckhardt performance will most likely be at the concert, and I'd like to see him jealous of you again. Wolfi, you will improvise on the melody you composed yesterday and play a concerto for violin and clavier. Is that clear? Now quickly go upstairs and get ready. I've hired three sedan chairs to take us to Mass and they will soon be here."

Since Wolfi was the smallest, he shared a sedan chair with Mama, and Papa and Nannerl each rode separately. Nannerl bumped along the driveway to the Palace of Versailles in the little box, looking out at the back of the carrier. She looked over and saw Wolfi on Mama's lap, making a face at her. She gave him a dignified wave and turned forward again. She wondered what the carriers thought about all day as they toted people around Versailles in sedan chairs.

They let her off at the royal chapel. Wolfi ran over to her while Papa was paying the drivers.

"C'mon," he said, pulling her arm. "Let's explore!" They ran over to a fountain that rose out of a huge pool. Nannerl counted twelve smaller fountains forming a circle around the huge centre fountain. Dim lights from the chapel flickered over the soft splash of moving water.

Wolfi dug around in the pocket of his vest, fished out a small, rusty coin and held it up to the light. "Remember, Nannerl?" he said. "Remember, Christmas Eve is the night for looking into the future and making sure that it's good? Let's toss something into the fountain and make a wish!" He squeezed his eyes tight for a while and then flung his coin. Nannerl could hear the soft plop of it sinking into the black water. "Hurry, Nannerl, make a wish!" he urged.

Nannerl searched through her pockets for a coin. Nothing. But then she felt a thin ring on her finger. It was the one she had found in her birthday cake, the one that had predicted she would marry. She pulled it off, held it up, took a deep breath and closed her eyes. She thought of Sopherl not playing the violin for twenty-five years. She remembered the thundering organ at night in the church at Wasserburg and the way it had felt to improvise for the Elector. She felt a pulse in her veins, winding all through her arms and legs and into her head. That was the music, wanting to get out somehow. Music ... that was all she wished for. To always let people hear her music, however she wanted — with the violin or her voice or a symphony....

"C'mon, Nannerl, throw it before Papa calls us to Mass," Wolfi interrupted her thoughts.

Nannerl opened her eyes and threw the ring with all her strength. She saw it flash like a tiny, golden bolt of lightning and disappear into the pool. Then she felt Mama's strong hand on her shoulder.

"Come now, to Mass," Mama whispered. "It's about to begin."

Nannerl followed Mama and Wolfi into the chapel. It was even fancier than the big cathedral in Salzburg; she

looked up and saw that the ceiling was covered in paintings. But even though it was beautiful, all she really
wanted was for the Mass to be over so that she could get
back to the room and start copying parts. The priest's
voice droned in her ears. She kneeled on the hard board
and stood and then kneeled again. She said the words but
she wasn't thinking about them. Everything became a
blur of candlelight and kneeling and fuzzy words ... then
the thin, tasteless crunch of the communion wafer and
the sour taste of wine and then more words. Over, over
... if only it were over. Nannerl's stomach rumbled and
her head whirled and she felt like fainting. But then the
great organ sounded through the chapel and cleared her
head. They walked into the cold night, where drivers
with sedan chairs waited to take people back to their
apartments.

She stared hard at her driver's back and wished that he
would hurry. She stared at his legs and his feet, wanting
them to run, to fly ... over the trees and the fountains, to
the hotel room and her symphony. When they finally
arrived, she saw by the big clock outside that it was past
midnight. She raced up to the room and got straight into
the little bed behind the partition. Mama stroked her hair
and kissed her forehead. "Goodnight, Nannerl, and a
Merry Christmas to my daughter," she said.

After everybody had said goodnight and wished each

other Merry Christmas, Nannerl crept out from underneath the covers and sat on the floor. She lit her fattest candle and fished under the bed for her symphony and the manuscript paper she had pinched from the stack Papa kept with the music books. Then she dipped her pen in ink and began to copy. Some of the Kerpens could share music, so in total she would just have to copy six parts, plus one for the organ. Her stomach grew tight — she still had to ask Wolfi!

It wasn't very hard, since the thinking work had already been done. It was just a matter of concentrating enough not to make a silly mistake like skipping a line of music in the flute part or dribbling black ink over a clean page. After a few hours she looked with satisfaction at five neatly copied parts; the flute, the two violin parts, the viola, the cello and the clavier. She yawned and lit a new candle and began on the organ part. She shifted her legs to get rid of a cramp. Her fingers and back and neck ached. She looked longingly at the soft mound of quilt above her and rested her head for a moment on the cold floor. Her eyelids drooped. No! She jerked herself awake and opened her eyes wide. She musn't fall asleep or she wouldn't get the parts copied and then she would have to play the Eckhardt sonata instead of her symphony!

She copied music until the black notes seemed to slide from her pen without effort. She fell into a rhythm;

dip, look at score, copy note, dip, look at score.... She told herself stories to keep herself awake. She remembered the ones Mama used to tell about Christmas Eve — how some people thought there was magic in the air on this night; trees flowered and gave fruit, mountains split open and flashed rubies and diamonds, animals sang to each other and church bells rang from the deep ocean. Somewhere a distant clock struck four and Nannerl worked faster.

She thought her fingers would drop off by the time she came to the violin duet in the finale. What if she couldn't play the violin after all? The lesson with Sopherl seemed like a far-away dream. And she hadn't even asked Wolfi for his violin yet! Something kept her fingers around the pen, kept her dipping it in the inkwell, kept her copying until she had filled in the final note. Then she spread the sheets out to dry. She wanted to write in her diary. The clock had just struck five, but she wanted to write about this — just a short note.

She tiptoed to the night table and opened the drawer. It wasn't there. The bottom of her stomach seemed to fall away as she tried to remember the last time she had seen the diary ... it was the night after Sopherl. Last night? Two nights ago? She couldn't remember. She got on her knees to search under the bed. But this time when her cheek rested on the cold floor she let it stay there. Then sleep pulled her away to dreams where loose pages of her diary and her symphony lay scattered over dark muddy streets and Wolfi and Johann Christian Bach wouldn't stop laughing.

The Christmas Day Concert

"Merry Christmas, Nannerl ... Nannerl!" a soft voice whispered into her ear and a hand shook her shoulder. She forced her eyelids open and saw Wolfi's wide blue eyes.

"What time is — " she started to say, but Wolfi held a finger to his lips and helped her to her feet. Her head throbbed and she felt like falling to the floor again. Her arms and neck felt stiff and cramped. She lay down on the bed and Wolfi jumped up and sat across from her.

"It's six o'clock and Mama and Papa are still sleeping," he whispered, moving closer to her on the bed. Nannerl rubbed her eyes and tried to keep them from closing. Wolfi looked as if he had something important to say. He picked at the quilt for a while and finally took her diary from the pocket of his vest. His face got red as he handed it to her.

So that's where her diary had been! "Wolfi, how could you — "

"I only read one page, the last one about your symphony and then I stopped, honest," he whispered. "I took it that night after I got back from the Mass with Papa. I'm sorry. I just wanted to do something mean to you for ... for hating me. You never ever hated me before." His lip quivered a bit and he squinted his eyes to hide his tears.

Nannerl wanted to say that she didn't hate him, that she had meant it when she had rapped "sorry" on the bench yesterday. But the jealous ache was stuck so tight in her throat she couldn't even whisper. Wolfi's small hands shook. Nannerl swallowed the awful ache and grabbed his hands in hers.

"Oh, Wolfi, of course I don't hate you," she finally managed to whisper. "I only said that because I was jealous that Johann Christian Bach thought you were so great and then laughed at me." She swallowed and hesitated and then blurted out, "I guess I get jealous of you a lot. I get jealous of how everyone pays attention to you all the time."

Wolfi looked at her with wide eyes. "Herr Bach laughed at you?"

Nannerl nodded. "When I asked him to listen to my symphony."

"Well, he should have listened," whispered Wolfi, hopping down from the bed. He began to turn red again. "I looked at your symphony before you woke up. It's incredible! I can hardly wait to hear it!" He turned around and looked at her. "Nannerl, could I play the organ part, please, please, please?"

Nannerl put her hand over her mouth and giggled. "Of course, silly. And can I borrow your violin, please, please, please? I need it for the concert and I need to practise, too!"

"It'll be a little small but I think you'll like it. Wait till I tell Papa about your symphony!"

Nannerl shook her head. "No. Please, Wolfi. Please don't tell Papa. That's something that I have to do, somehow."

Wolfi nodded and tiptoed away, and Nannerl got under her quilt and slipped back into dreams.

· — · —

"Now children," Papa instructed over lunch. "When you see the King and Queen and members of the royal family you must not kiss their hands or even bow but stand straight and let them pass by. That is the custom here and we don't want anyone to think that we Germans don't know any better."

"But Papa, the Empress Maria Theresa herself took me on her lap and kissed me," said Wolfi, shoving a piece of bread in his mouth.

"That was in Vienna, Wolfi," said Papa. "Here we

must not kiss or talk to them. That is the custom of the court."

Nannerl reached for another piece of marzipan. She didn't feel a bit tired. Mama had let them sleep in late, and in the morning, as a Christmas treat to break the fast, Mama had set out plates of marzipan, almonds, *Pfeffernüsse* and chocolates. Now they were almost gone.

"You'd better save some room for the feast at Versailles," said Mama as Nannerl took the last chocolate. She put it back on the plate, went to her wardrobe and took out her rose satin performance dress, tracing her finger along the lace and hoping for luck. She had actually managed to practise the violin for an hour, when Mama and Papa had been out for a walk. The duet part at the end of the symphony really wasn't too hard.

Now Mama spent a long time pulling Nannerl's corset tight and fussing with her wig. "Hurry or we'll be late," Papa called from the doorway. Nannerl quickly stuck the pages of her symphony inside the book of Eckhardt sonatas. The clock struck three as Mama and Wolfi and Nannerl finally rushed after Papa, down the long stairway to the street below. Papa paced back and forth, twisting his hands.

"Where are all the sedan chairs when we need them?" he said as he paced. "The banquet is to begin at four o' clock and we simply cannot be late."

They waited and waited, but every sedan chair that passed them had a passenger.

"This is ridiculous!" Papa shouted as he looked at his watch for what seemed like the fiftieth time. Nannerl began to think they wouldn't get there and that her symphony would always stay silent.

"I see some empty sedan chairs!" shouted Wolfi, jumping up and down and waving his arms to get the attention of the drivers who had just rounded the corner. Papa promised them extra money if they ran as fast as they could to Versailles.

Nannerl began to go over the symphony in her head as soon as she was seated in the sedan chair box alone. What if Sopherl hadn't been able to get the message to the Kerpens? What if they hadn't brought their instruments? She couldn't worry about that now. She imagined picking up Wolfi's violin and putting it under her chin. She could imagine the surprised look on Papa's face. She really should warn him ahead of time, but then he would just tell her not to play it, or worse: he would laugh.

Halfway down the long driveway to the Palace of Versailles it began to rain. Nannerl saw the front driver look up at the dark clouds and run faster. She squinted out the window at the sleety rain, glimpsing wide gardens and fountains and rows of grey buildings that seemed to go on for miles. Finally, they entered the large front gates into the main courtyard and the drivers stopped in front of a set of wide doors. Nannerl tucked the book with her symphony under her cape, ducked her head against the rain, and made a run for the entrance.

Papa, Wolfi and Mama all arrived inside behind her, breathless and damp. A guard came towards them, smiling. He spoke in Swiss German: "You are late. But I have special orders from the Queen herself to bring you straight to the banquet, to her table!" They followed him through a maze of hallways to a huge room crowded with guests. Nannerl felt like sinking down through the floor as everyone turned to stare at them. As she walked, she glimpsed the faces of Charlotte and Baron Kerpen, and of Johann Christian Bach. Everyone seemed to be here! She scanned the crowd again, hoping to see Sopherl.

When they reached the grand head table where the royal family sat, the guard took Wolfi to stand in the position of honour, directly behind the Queen. Papa stood next to Wolfi behind the King, and Mama and Nannerl stood beside Papa behind two women in fancy dresses.

"So, would my little man like some duck?" Nannerl could hear the Queen's voice above the din in the hall. Wolfi's curls bobbed up and down and the Queen passed him a plate of steaming food.

"Thank you very much!" said Wolfi, taking her hands

to kiss them. Papa began to shake his head but the Queen just laughed.

"The little wonder boy shall kiss my hands as much as he likes!" she announced.

"Could I have some of that chocolate as well, please?" asked Wolfi.

"Wolfgang!" Papa began to scold, but the Queen just laughed and passed Wolfi a huge plate of chocolates.

One lady passed Nannerl some duck. It was different than anything she'd ever tasted — sweet, with some kind of creamy sauce. She licked her fingers and shifted her feet and wished that the tight feeling in her stomach would go away. Papa seemed to think it was such an honour to stand behind the Royal family but she just wanted to sit like everybody else! If only she could play her symphony and get it all over with!

Finally, the King stood and cleared his throat. The hall suddenly became quiet. "I am sure that we are all waiting for the gala Christmas Day concert. I have been anticipating it for many weeks and am especially looking forward to hearing the celebrated children of Mozart, from Salzburg!" There was a great roar of applause and Nannerl felt her hands go clammy and cold. The King banged his cup on the table for silence. "We will all meet in the grand music hall in precisely half an hour to witness the great event!" Applause sounded again.

As she filed out of the banquet room behind Mama, Nannerl noticed Charlotte Kerpen trying to catch her attention by pretending to play the flute. Nannerl smiled at her and waved. Sopherl must have got the message to them after all! The knot in her stomach loosened a bit.

"Wolfi and Nannerl, stay close to Mama and me so you don't get lost in the crowd on the way," Papa said, resting his hands lightly on their shoulders. Nannerl nodded and for a while they all stayed together, but she kept getting ahead. She walked fast because it helped to get rid of some of the tightness in her chest and stomach and throat. Soon she was far from Wolfi and Mama and Papa, alone in the crowd, pushing through the maze of rooms and hallways leading to the music hall and the performance of her symphony. She stopped suddenly under a huge archway and caught her breath.

The hall of mirrors stretched before her. All the way along the left side were huge, arching mirrors that almost touched the curved ceiling covered in paintings. They reflected the light of what seemed like hundreds of candles. Nannerl gingerly made her way down the polished floor, feeling that she was walking through a huge fireplace, with all the dancing shadows and pools of light reflected off the mirrors. She glanced at her reflection. She looked hunched and tight with the spooky light flickering over her face. She took a deep breath and brought her shoulders back and walked on through the passage with the sound of her symphony pulsing inside her.

At last she reached the music hall with its grand organ. Her heart beat hard as she stood in the doorway and looked over the crowds of people. She had never played for such a huge audience!

"There you are, Nannerl!" said Mama, taking her arm. "You shouldn't have wandered off — we thought you were lost. You gave us a scare."

"I'm fine, Mama, really," said Nannerl. She noticed with relief that Papa was too busy to scold; he was securing front-row seats. They sat down just as the music director got up to make the introductions.

"We are pleased to have such honoured guests at our Christmas Day concert...." he began. He looked as if he might talk for quite a while. Nannerl sighed and squirmed in her seat. If only she could play, now, before she lost the courage. It was the uncertainty of it all that made her heart pound. What if Papa became so angry that he threw her out on the street to live with the beggars in the shadow of Nôtre Dame? She felt the steady rise and fall of Papa's breath beside her and the soft brush of his coat. She wanted him to be proud of her ... maybe she should just forget about her symphony and play the Eckhardt.

"... and Mozart will now introduce his prodigies," finished the music director and sat down. Papa took a deep breath and faced the audience.

"Honoured guests of the court of Versailles," he began. Nannerl noticed that his hand was shaking. "I'm sure you've all heard of my son, Wolfgang Amadeus ... now, at long last, you will hear the music. Honoured guests, may I introduce Wolfgang Amadeus Mozart, future musical director of the courts of Europe!"

Wolfi trotted up to the clavier and bowed to the huge applause. He stroked the keys and his melodies soared up to the great chandeliers and danced there with the hundreds of candles in warmth and light. As she listened, Nannerl felt all the queasiness slip from her stomach and slither across the polished floor. She didn't feel a rotten ache any more when she listened to Wolfi play. The notes tickled her skin like Bimberl's fur and made her want to laugh and get up on her chair and dance.

When he was finished, the audience roared for more and he played a concerto for violin and clavier. Nannerl watched the bow and his fingers and longed to have her own turn. Yet she dreaded it, too. What if she made mistakes? She felt the queasiness return as Wolfi neared the end of the third movement.

After the thunder of applause for Wolfi, Papa stood to introduce her.

"My eleven year old daughter, Maria Anna, will now execute, with amazing precision, a sonata by Johann Gottfried Eckhardt."

Nannerl saw the gleam in his eye as he sat down. She walked to the front of the hall to the applause, deciding at the last minute to play the Eckhardt. That would be the safest thing. All she had to do was sit down at the clavier and play with precision and everyone would clap and be happy. That old composer would be jealous and Papa would be proud.

She sat down at the clavier and poised her hands above the keys as a hush settled in the great hall. Those two voices fought inside her. One urged her to go ahead and play the Eckhardt. The other one told her not to worry about what they thought and to get up and lead her symphony. *Who cares what they think, as long as you know that it's the best thing you ever wrote.* Katherl's words echoed in her head.

She had to perform her symphony. She had to try. Nannerl took a big breath and stood up to face the crowd, her knees trembling under her thick dress. A wave of whispers and coughing went through the audience.

"I am not going to play the Eckhardt tonight," she said, her voice sounding dim yellow and thin. She looked straight at Papa and saw a flush creep over his face. He looked at the floor. "I am going to perform a symphony which I have composed ... some friends will help me ... the Kerpen family orchestra ..." There was a clatter of chairs at the back as the Kerpens stood and got out their instruments. "And my own brother, Wolfi, playing the organ."

She pulled the parts from the pages of the Eckhardt book and passed them out to the Kerpens as they walked to the front. She showed Franz Kerpen the duet part in the last movement. Then she grabbed Wolfi's violin and gave them an A to tune up, just as the concertmaster of the Mannheim orchestra had done. She was running down a hill and there was no way she could stop now. She lifted the scroll of the violin for the upbeat and they were off.

She loved the feel of the wood against her neck, and the way her bow sank into the string and pulled out notes like shiny rocks from the sand. But even more, she loved the way all the different melodies swirled around her; the trills like sweets from the Baron Kerpen's flute, the distant thunder of Wolfi's organ, the violins and the cello and the clavier like wind, mixing it all together.

Nannerl stood with Franz for the violin duet in the finale and closed her eyes as she played. She didn't care if she was playing for the King and Queen of France or the beggars at Nôtre Dame; it was this music spilling out from inside her that mattered. She listened to Franz' violin ... it sounded different, somehow. She opened her eyes and saw that he was standing back and that Sopherl had taken his place! She had come after all! Their violins danced together by the light of the Wasserburg moon, sang out from the tops of fountains and hedges, jumped through the air and landed with the final note of the symphony on top of the Salzburg mountains.

It seemed to Nannerl that the crowd was silent for hours. Then a man near the back stood and clapped and shouted bravo! The audience rose suddenly like a huge wave. The cheers and applause filled Nannerl's ears until she thought they would burst. She noticed Mama clapping with a little smile and Papa ... Papa came forward with tears in the corners of his eyes.

The audience was soon milling about, chatting and calling for coats. The Queen and the King's daughters came over and kissed Nannerl and Wolfi and laughingly gave Nannerl a heavy toothpick case of solid gold and a tortoiseshell snuffbox and Wolfi a gold snuffbox and a tiny gold watch. Sopherl came to give Nannerl a big hug.

"How can I thank you?" asked Nannerl.

"No, it's you that I thank," she answered. She took Nannerl's arm and led her back to the clavier.

"Play something with me? There's a little farewell tune the Elector and I used to play at Nymphenburg, at the end of our evenings of music-making — " Sopherl began to play softly.

Nannerl listened closely. It was as if the violin were Sopherl's real voice, her speaking voice just a foreign language she was forced to use sometimes. It was a simple tune, just a few sentences, and after listening for a while, Nannerl got out Wolfi's violin and started to play. The din in the room began to quiet. Out of the corner of her eye, Nannerl could see people sitting back down in their chairs.

After a few rounds of the tune Nannerl started adding notes, thanking Sopherl for the violin lesson and for playing in her symphony. Sopherl answered back with a quick little scale, like a laugh. Nannerl held the end note a little longer to ask Sopherl a question, and a clavier joined in.

The audience had stopped talking. The hall was quiet, everyone listening to the small group at the front. A cello joined, and some more violins. Nannerl looked around and saw that the Kerpens and Wolfi and even Papa were playing the sad, slow tune around and around them. A circle of music — and she and Sopherl played in the middle of it.

Nannerl didn't want it to end. But after a while she felt a tug. She knew she would have to say goodbye, the way she'd said goodbye to Katherl and the Salzburg mountains, to Charlotte in Coblenz, to each inn and palace and clock and church. She played one last note for Sopherl and let her bow come to a stop on the string.

The audience burst into applause. Nannerl bowed and then looked over at Sopherl. She just smiled — her eyes were still a bit sad and secret — and packed up her violin. People were starting to come forward with congratulations. Sopherl gave Nannerl's hand one last squeeze and before anyone could stop her, quietly left the room.

Nannerl wanted to run after her, make her stop and play some more music. But something in her said that wouldn't work. She would just have to wait. Some day she'd meet Sopherl again, maybe in another symphony.

"I wonder where that haunting tune came from?" Charlotte was saying, as the Kerpens and even Herr Bach crowded around to talk about the symphony and Sopherl's melody. The adults talked and talked. Nannerl began to feel her eyelids droop. She wanted to curl up in front of a fire and sleep for days and days.

At last it was time to leave. When she, Mama, Wolfi and Papa finally walked through the big doors of the music hall into the Christmas night, the sleet had turned to snow: Nannerl felt a big, wet, flake on her forehead.

"Snow!" screamed Wolfi and raced ahead, jumping up and trying to catch the heavy flakes on his tongue. Nannerl ran after him and tried to catch them too; they giggled and ran in circles with their faces to the sky.

Mama and Papa caught up to them. They stared up

at the snow and Mama linked her arm in Papa's. "Grandma Pertl used to say that when the weather was cold at Christmas, the winter would be hard but spring would come early," she said.

"This spring we shall be in London," said Papa. "I know my wonderful children will take that city by storm. I was very proud of both of you tonight."

Nannerl shivered, although she didn't feel a bit cold. She grabbed Wolfi's hand and together they raced and skipped and danced ahead. She ran with all her might, looking at the sky and humming a new melody, a song of spring.

Author's Note

While *The Secret Wish of Nannerl Mozart* is a work of fiction, Nannerl was a real person, and much of this novel is drawn from real events in her life. My research for this novel came from many books, but two of the most useful were the letters that Leopold Mozart, Nannerl's father, wrote to their landlord, Lorenz Hagenauer, during the 1763 – 1766 Grand Tour, and a biography of Nannerl written in German by Eva Rieger. A List of Sources is included for readers who want to learn more about Nannerl.

The dates of the major life events for Nannerl and Wolfi are listed in the book's Chronology. In the novel, I changed the date of Nannerl's real birthday to accommodate the Mozarts' travel schedule. A number of the documents that I have mentioned are real. You can still find *Notebook for Nannerl* in music stores or at the library if you would like to learn the minuets that Leopold Mozart composed to teach Nannerl how to play the clavier. The book is complete with Leopold's notes on Wolfi's progress written at the bottom of some of the pieces.

Nannerl's diary is also real. For many years she kept a diary which Wolfi sometimes shared. The diary entries in this novel, however, are all imagined. The diary was eventually inherited by Wolfgang's widow. Unfortunately, she didn't realize its importance. She lost pages, or cut them up and gave them away to friends and collectors. Those pages that remained were gathered together and published in German.

The newspaper excerpt praising Wolfi and Nannerl is a translation of an actual article written by Melchoir Grimm, the famous editor of the *Correspondance littéraire*, a literary journal read by many European intellectuals.

The children's dog and doll are also mentioned in the historical accounts. The Mozarts had a fox terrier who was named Bimberl. The children seemed fond of pet names: Bimberl was also nicknamed Pimperl, Miss Bimbes or Miss Pimsess. The doll, Salome Musch, was named after the family cook. Years after the children had stopped playing with it, the doll was brought down from the attic and given to Nannerl's son to play with.

Besides the Mozart family, many of the other characters in the novel are also historical. Katherl really was a friend of Nannerl's. Her full name was Maria Anna Katharina Gilowsky, and she was the eldest daughter of the Salzburg court surgeon, Andreas Gilowsky. Johann Christian Bach (1735 – 1782), was the son of the famous Johann Sebastian Bach. The meeting in Paris, however, is invented. The Mozarts didn't actually meet Johann

Christian Bach until they reached London, where the prominent and popular composer had a great influence on Wolfi's style of writing music.

Many of the other musicians mentioned are also historical. Johann Baptist Wendling (1723 – 1797) was a famous flautist who played in the Mannheim orchestra. Wolfi and Nannerl played a concert at Schwetzingen Palace with the Mannheim orchestra on July 19, 1763. Johann Schobert (1735 – 1767) was a composer and famous player of the harpsichord. He actually did express his jealousy of Nannerl's precise and excellent playing of very difficult pieces by Johann Gottfried Eckhardt (1735 – 1809), another composer. When in Coblenz, the Mozarts spent a good deal of time with the family of the Baron Kerpen. His seven sons and two daughters all played one or two instruments — the clavier, violin, cello — or sang.

In addition, many of the details I have recounted of the events of the Mozarts' tour I discovered in historical documents, particularly in Leopold Mozart's letters. During their first musical tour, in 1762, the Mozarts visited Schönbrunn Palace in Vienna, home of the Empress Maria Theresa. Leopold Mozart writes, in a letter of October 16, 1762, that Wolfi "jumped up on the Empress' lap, put his arms round her neck and kissed her heartily." He tells about the broken wheel in his letter of June 11, 1763. And the Mozarts *were* stranded in Wasserburg, where Wolfi tried the organ for the first time. Nannerl's organ concert is, however, imagined.

You can still visit Nymphenburg Palace in Munich. At the Mozarts' concert for Maximilian the Third, Elector of Bavaria, they actually did run out of time for Nannerl because Wolfi used up all the time improvising and playing a concerto for violin and clavier. Leopold mentions in his letter of June 21, 1763, that "the Elector said twice that he was sorry not to have heard my little girl." Because of the Elector's comments, Nannerl went back to Nymphenburg to play for the Elector where she was "warmly applauded." The Mozarts met Maria Sophia, sister of the Elector, at the dinner at Nymphenburg. (The rest of Sopherl's story is imagined.)

The little portable clavier was purchased from J. A. Stein in Augsburg so that Wolfi and Nannerl could practise on their travels. The Mozarts arrived at Versailles on Christmas Eve, 1763, and were invited to a public court dinner on New Year's Day. Leopold writes that Wolfi "was requested to stand all the while beside the Queen, to talk constantly with her and entertain her, and frequently to kiss her hands, and to eat right beside her of the dishes which she graciously handed to him from the table [...] I stood by him, and on the King's other side [...] stood my wife and daughter."

The restrictions imposed on young girls and women

that are recounted in this novel are true. Both the organ and the violin were seen as instruments to be used by men working as professional directors of music in courts or churches. Since women were never allowed to hold such jobs, girls were not encouraged to play the organ or the violin, or to learn composition or improvisation. Leopold Mozart gave these lessons to Wolfi but not to Nannerl. Nannerl was given lessons in playing the clavier, with and without the keyboard covered by a cloth, and in singing. Though none of Nannerl's compositions were published, we do know that she composed pieces for the organ and clavier.

CHRONOLOGY

July 30, 1751: Maria Anna Walburga Ignatia Mozart is born.

January 27, 1756: Wolfgang Amadeus Mozart is born.

January 1762 – January 1763: The first tour of the Mozart family through Austria.

June 1763 – November 1766: The grand tour through Munich, Augsburg, the Rhine, Aachen and Brussels to Paris and Versailles; to London for over a year, back through Holland, through Switzerland and Bavaria.

> *June 1763:* Wasserburg, Munich
> *July 1763:* Ludwigsburg, Schwetzingen Palace
> *September 1763:* Rhine journey, Coblenz
> *October 1763:* Austrian Netherlands, Brussels
> *November 1763:* Paris
> *December 1763 – January 1764:* Versailles

September 1767 – January 1769: The second tour of Austria, Nannerl's last "prodigy" tour.

August 23, 1784: Nannerl marries Johann Baptist
   Berchtold zu Sonnenburg.

December 5, 1791: Wolfgang dies at age 35 in Vienna.

October 29, 1829: Nannerl dies at age 78 in Salzburg.

GLOSSARY

Baumkuchen: "Tree cake"; German Advent cake made to look like the cross-section of a tree trunk.

Cartwright: A person who repairs carts.

Christstollen: German Advent sweet yeast bread, coated with icing sugar and made to resemble the Christ child wrapped in swaddling clothes.

Clavier: Any musical instrument having a keyboard, especially a stringed keyboard instrument such as a harpsichord or clavichord.

Concertmaster: The leader of the first violins in an orchestra, who is usually the assistant to the conductor.

Concerto: A composition for one or more solo instruments, with orchestral accompaniment.

Forte: A direction in music which means "loud."

Gugelhupf: A fancy cake mould with a swirled or fluted pattern.

Kapellmeister: Director of music.

Marzipan: A candy made of almond paste with sugar that is moulded into various shapes.

Minuet: A piece of music written for the minuet, which is a slow, stately dance popular in the 17th and 18th centuries.

Motet: A vocal composition with many voices, intended for use in a church service.

Parallel Fifths: Two voice parts progressing, so that the interval (fifth) between them stays the same.

Pfeffernüsse: A German Christmas cookie with a gingerbread taste, made by rolling dough into strips and cutting it into small pieces.

Score: A piece of music with all the instrumental or vocal parts written on each page.

Sight-read: To play or sing a piece of music without previous practice.

Snuffbox: A small fancy box for holding ground tobacco.

Sonata: An extended instrumental composition, usually in several movements.

Sou: Either of two bronze coins of France.

Stops: Knobs which are drawn out or pushed back to control various parts of an organ.

Symphony: An instrumental composition in three or more movements, similar in form to a sonata but written for an orchestra.

Trill: A fast alteration of two notes which are very close.

Wunderkind: "Wonder child."

Zwölfjahrekerze: "Twelve year candle."

LIST OF SOURCES

Anderson, Emily, ed. and trans. *The Letters of Mozart and His Family*. London: Macmillan, 1938.

Buckalew, Martha Harter. "The Other Mozart," *Keyboard Classics* 9 (1989): 6-7.

Burney, Charles. *Music, Men and Manners in France and Italy 1770*. Ed. Edmund Poole. London: Eulenberg, 1974.

Hummel, Walter. "*Tagebuchblätter von Nannerl und Wolfgang Mozart*," *Mozart Jahrbuch des Zentralinstituts fur Mozartforschung* 1957: 207-211.

Hunter, Clarice. "Whatever Became of Nannerl Mozart?" *Clavier* April 1979: 30-31.

Hutchings, Arthur. *Mozart: The Man. The Musician*. New York: Schirmer, 1976.

Mozart, Leopold. *Notebook for Nannerl*. Ed. Hans Kann. Tokyo: Zen-On Music Company, Universal Edition No. 17145.

Perl, Lila. *Candles, Cakes, and Donkey Tails. Birthday Symbols and Celebrations.* New York: Clarion, 1984.

Rieger, Eva. *Nannerl Mozart: Leben einer Kunstlerin im 18. Jahrhundert.* Frankfurt am Main: Insel Verlag, 1990.

Russ, Jennifer M. *German Festivals and Customs.* London: Oswald Wolff, 1982.

Sadie, Stanley, ed. "Maria Anna (Walburga Ignatia) Mozart." In *The New Grove Dictionary of Music and Musicians.* London: Macmillan, 1980.

Schenk, Erich. *Mozart and His Times.* Eds. and trans. Richard and Clara Winston. New York: Alfred A. Knopf, 1959.

SECOND STORY PRESS

BOOKS FOR YOUNG READERS

A Friend Like Zilla   *Gilmore*

A Ghost in My Mirror   *Hébert*

A Monster in My Cereal   *Hébert*

Ezzie's Emerald   *McDonnell*

Fitting In   *Kirsh*

Hattie Pearl Click Click   *Hearn*

Jeremy and the Aunties   *Finn*

Katherine and the Garbage Dump   *Morris*

Poppy's Whale   *Hébert*

The Summer Kid   *Levy*

PICTURE BOOKS

Aunt Fred is a Witch   *Gilmore*

Being Big   *Liddell*

Franny and the Music Girl   *Hearn*

It's a Jungle in Here   *Bingham*

Lights for Gita   *Gilmore*

Roses for Gita   *Gilmore*

Sasha and the Wiggly Tooth   *Tregebov*

Sasha and the Wind   *Tregebov*

The Amazing Adventures of Littlefish   *Hébert*

The Extraordinary Ordinary Everything Room   *Tregebov*

Wheniwasalittlegirl   *Gilmore*

— *Bevan Voth*

BARBARA KATHLEEN NICKEL
is an award-winning poet who also
writes for young adults. Her book of
poetry, *The Gladys Elegies*, is published
by Coteau Books. Originally from
Saskatchewan, she now teaches violin
and writes in British Columbia.